It's So Funny, You'll Want Seconds!

by
ED FISCHER

Adventure Publications, Inc.
Cambridge, Minnesota

In more ways than one, lutefisk seems to have a life of its own.

Few other food items have enjoyed as much press as this pungent fish. Alternately awed and made fun of, lutefisk has withstood the test of time with all the personality it began with.

According to legend,* lutefisk originated when Jens Luteness came home with his catch of cod and, not having a place to hang them out to dry, stored them in a rain barrel filled with his wife's caustic wash water. The fish soaked (and stunk) for weeks. Jens finally checked on his cod and was surprised to see that they had not rotted away. It was at this point in time that the expression "ish da!" was born. Why Jens and his wife proceeded to cook and dine on the fish in this condition has not been fully explained. Since then, lutefisk (named after Jens Luteness) has been a traditional and endearing dish of Norwegians everywhere.

Like the cartoons in this book, lutefisk goes with joyful get-togethers, laughter and warm, cozy kitchens.

* From *Cream and Bread* by Janet Martin and Allen Todnem

Dedicated to Lavonne and all my Norwegian friends who are looking for other ways to use lutefisk.

Text and illustrations copyright 2002 by Ed Fischer

Book design by Jonathan Norberg

Published by Adventure Publications, Inc.
820 Cleveland Street South
Cambridge, MN 55008
1-800-678-7006

ISBN 1-885061-44-7

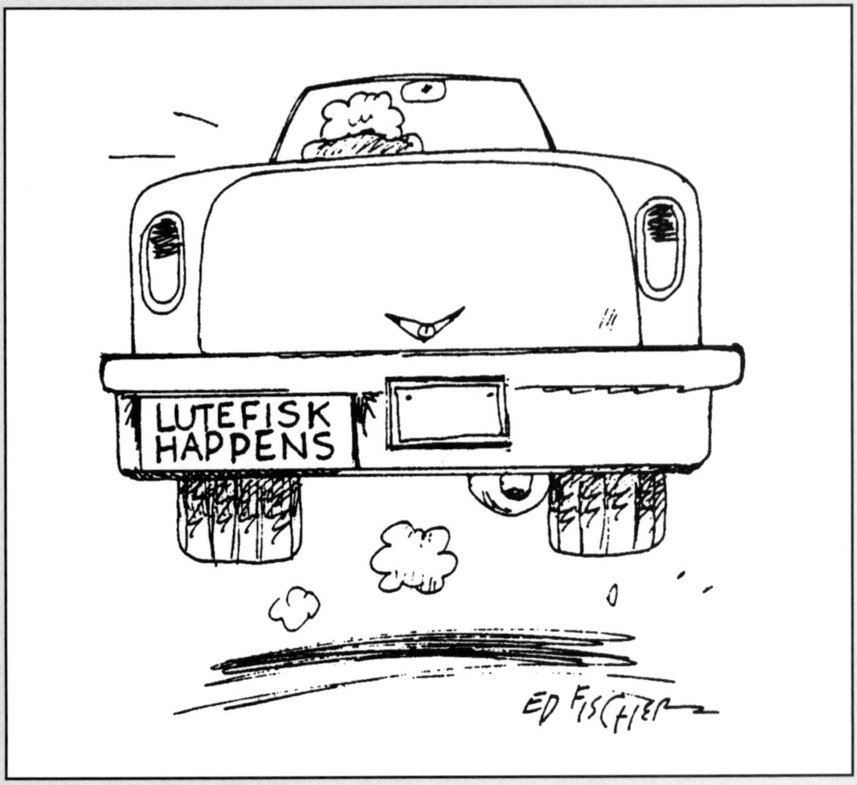
LUTEFISK
HAPPENS
ED FISCHER

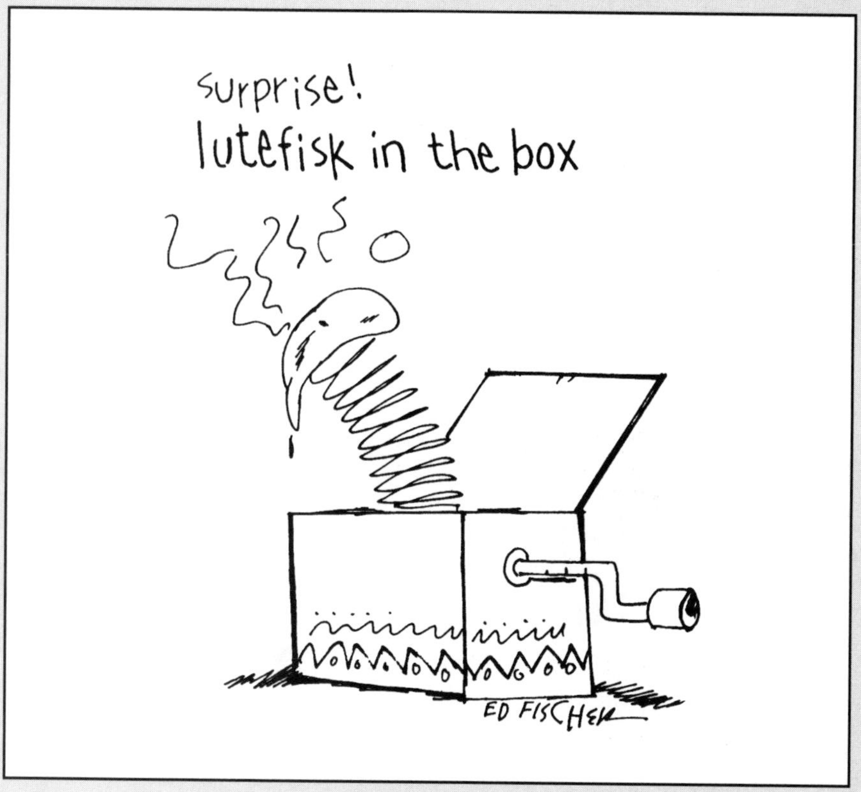
surprise!
lutefisk in the box
ED FISCHER

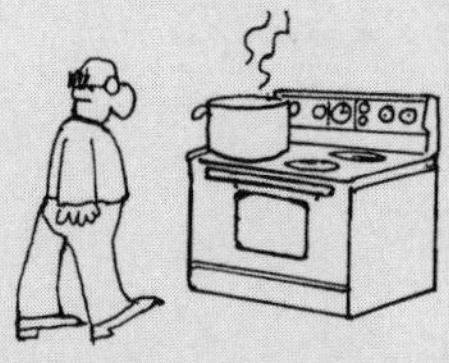

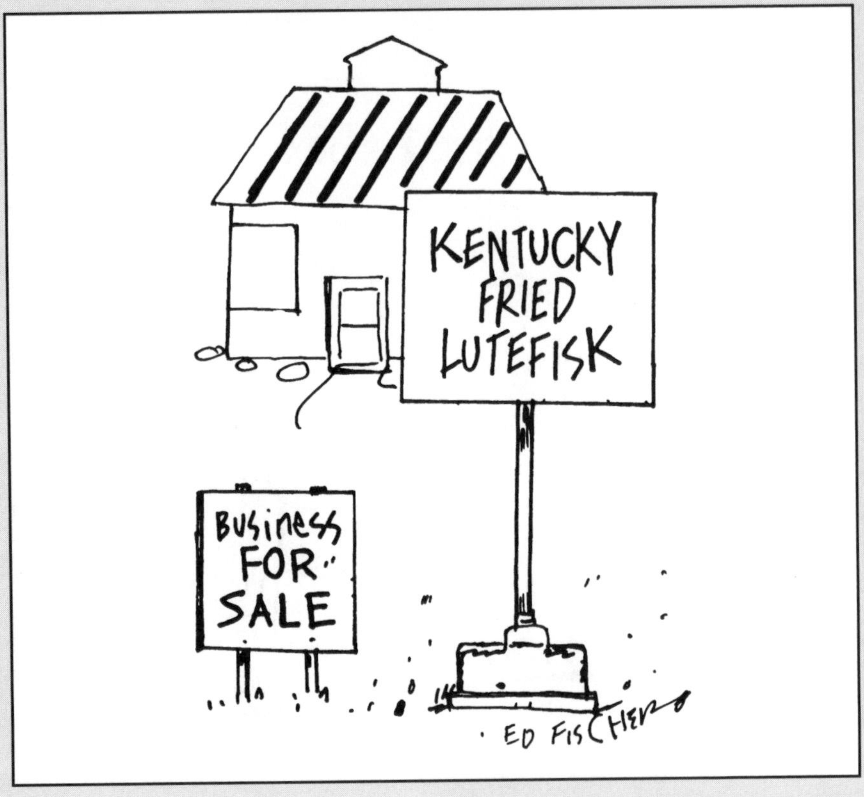
KENTUCKY
FRIED
LUTEFISK
Business
FOR
SALE
ED FISCHER

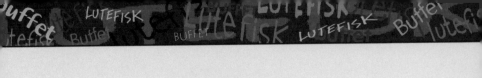

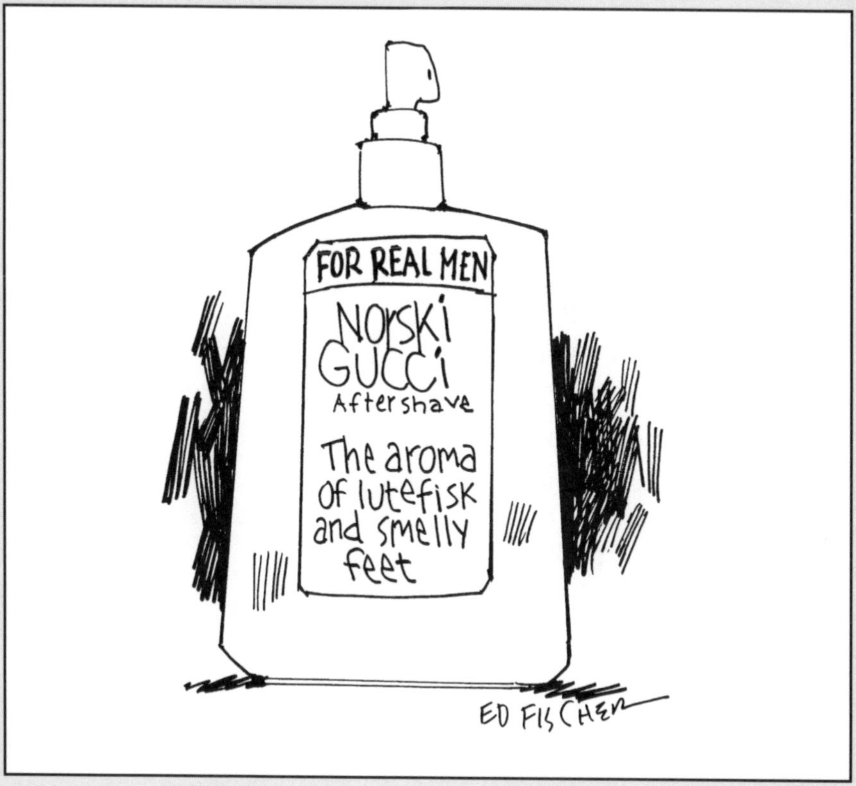
FOR REAL MEN
Norski Gucci Aftershave
The aroma of lutefisk and smelly feet
ED FISCHER

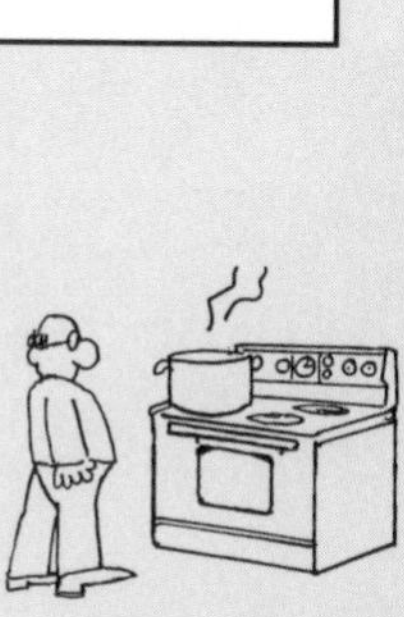

The oldest lutefisk recipe:

Saute lutefisk, carrots, potatoes and onions in butter and place on an old cedar board.

Grill for about one hour.

Throw out lutefisk and eat board and vegetables.

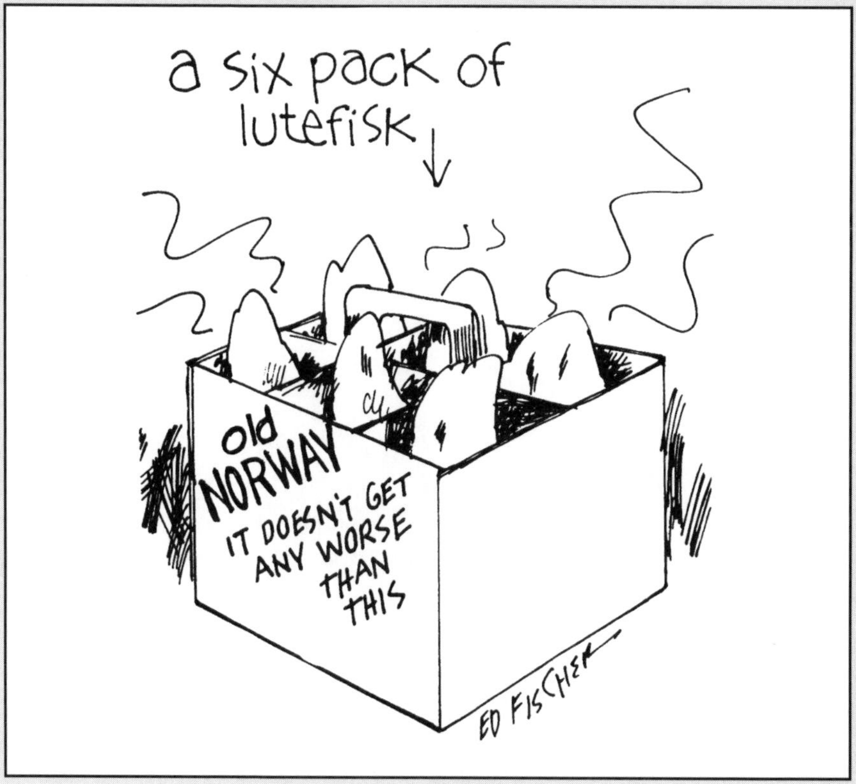
a six pack of lutefisk
old NORWAY
IT DOESN'T GET ANY WORSE THAN THIS
ED FISCHER

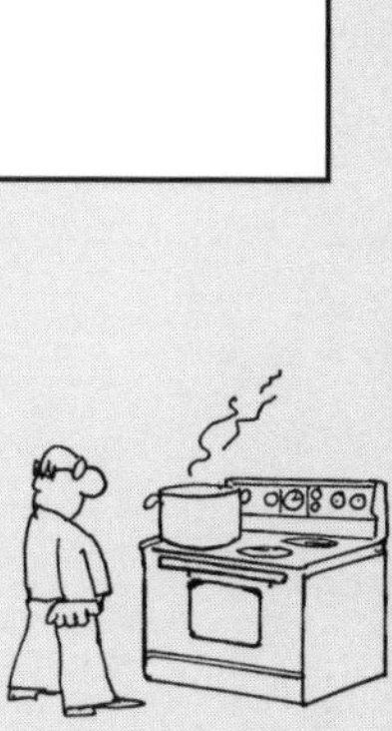

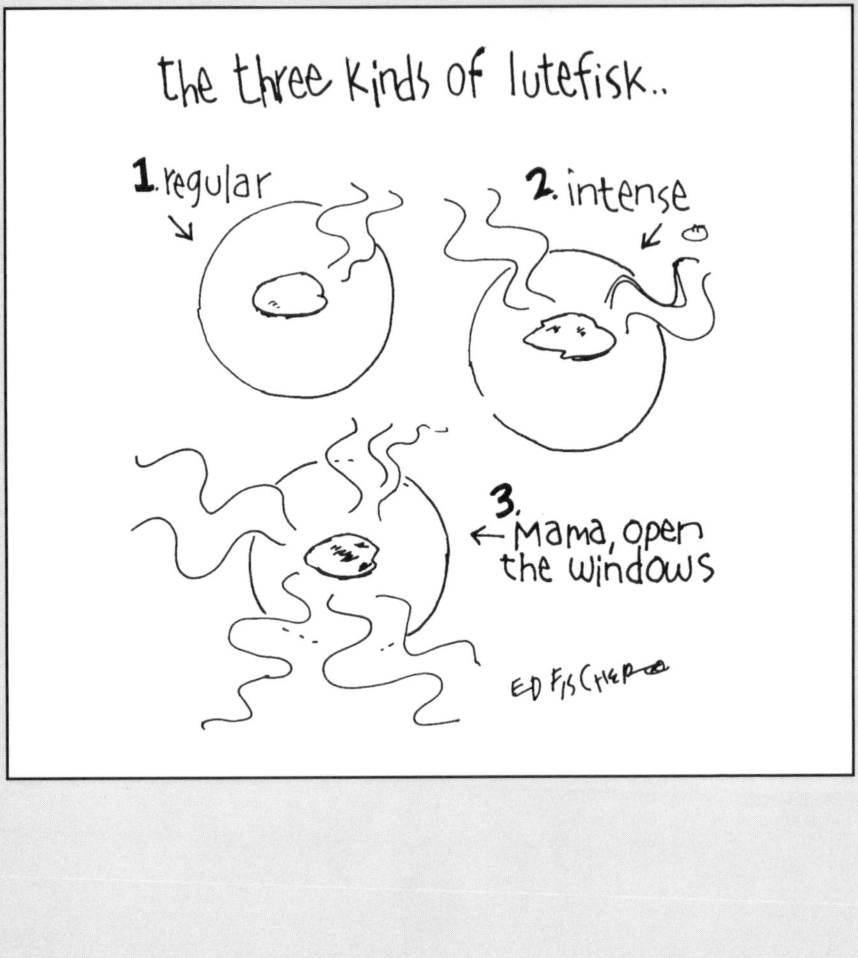
the three kinds of lutefisk..
1. regular
2. intense
3. ← Mama, open the windows
ED FISCHER

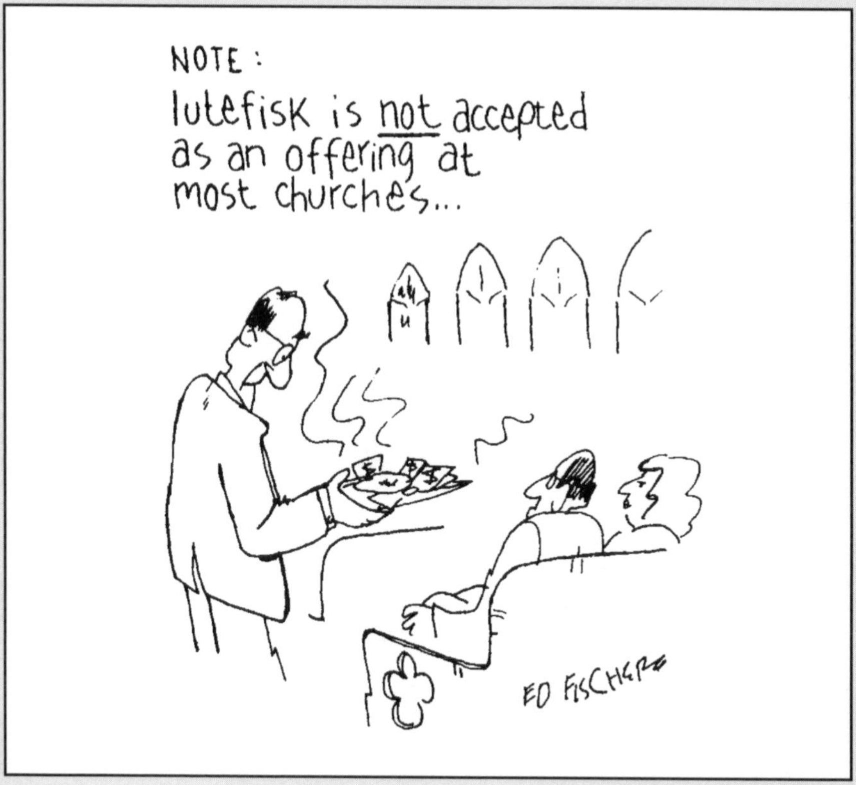
NOTE:
lutefisk is not accepted as an offering at most churches...
ED FISCHER

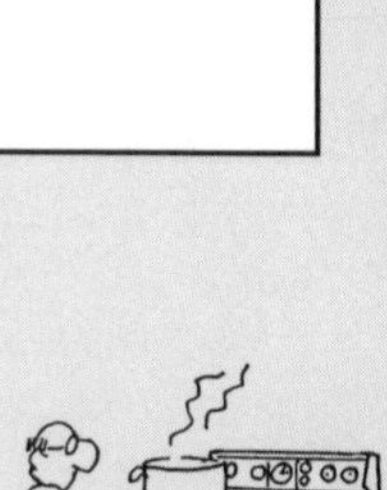

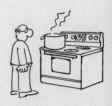

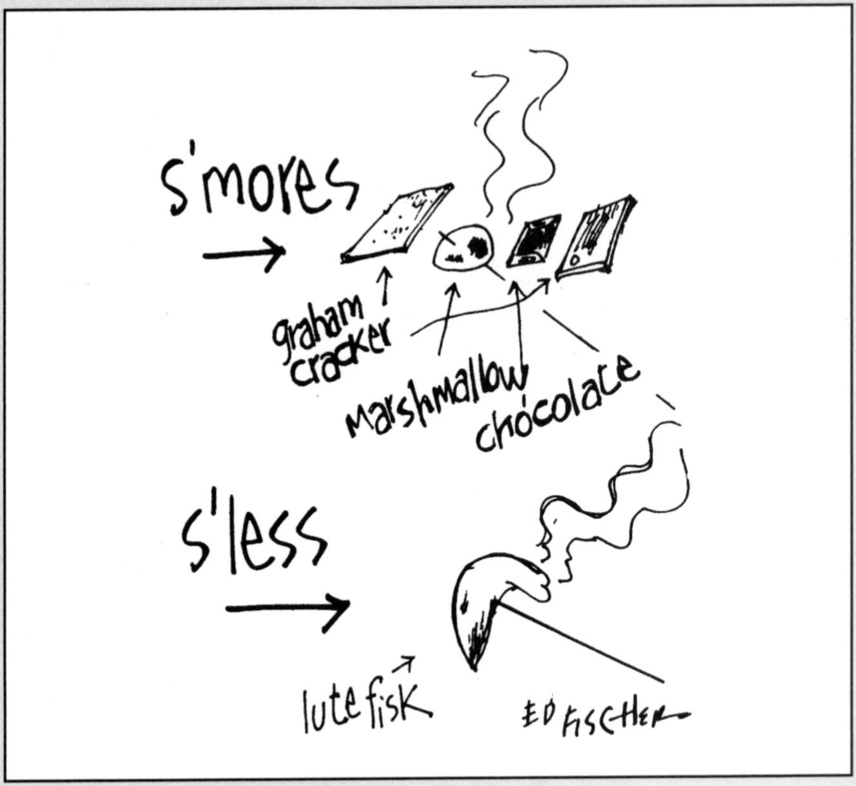
s'mores
graham cracker
marshmallow
chocolate
s'less
lutefisk
ED FISCHER

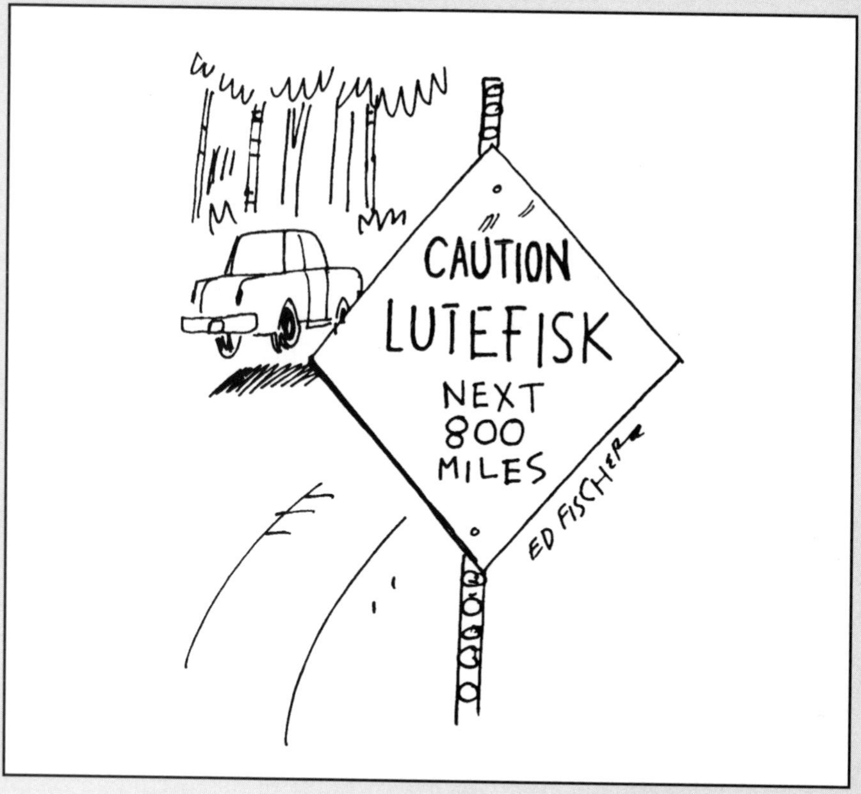
CAUTION
LUTEFISK
NEXT
800
MILES
ED FISCHER

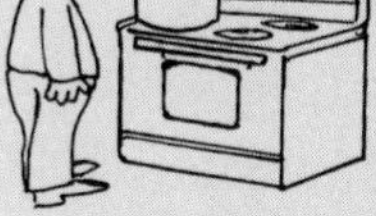

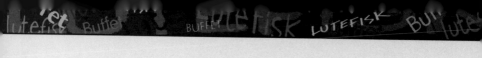

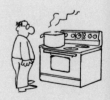

Though not Scandinavian, Gene Swartz of Rockdale, Minnesota, bought lutefisk to eat with friends. But after cooking it, they began to change their minds. Gene made a decision. "If the cat eats it," he said, "then we will too." The cat ate a bite and keeled over. It was only until later that they discovered the cat had just pretended to be dead.

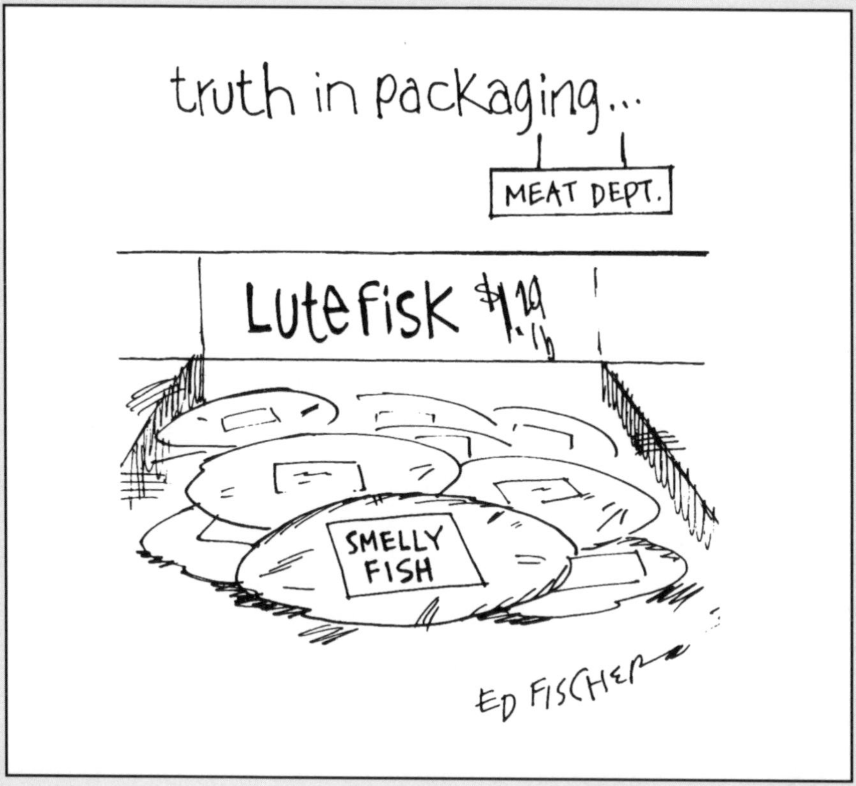
truth in packaging...
MEAT DEPT.
Lutefisk $1.19 lb
SMELLY FISH
ED FISCHER

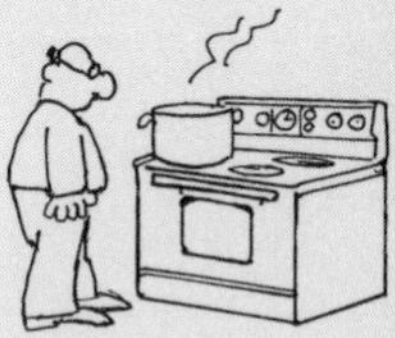

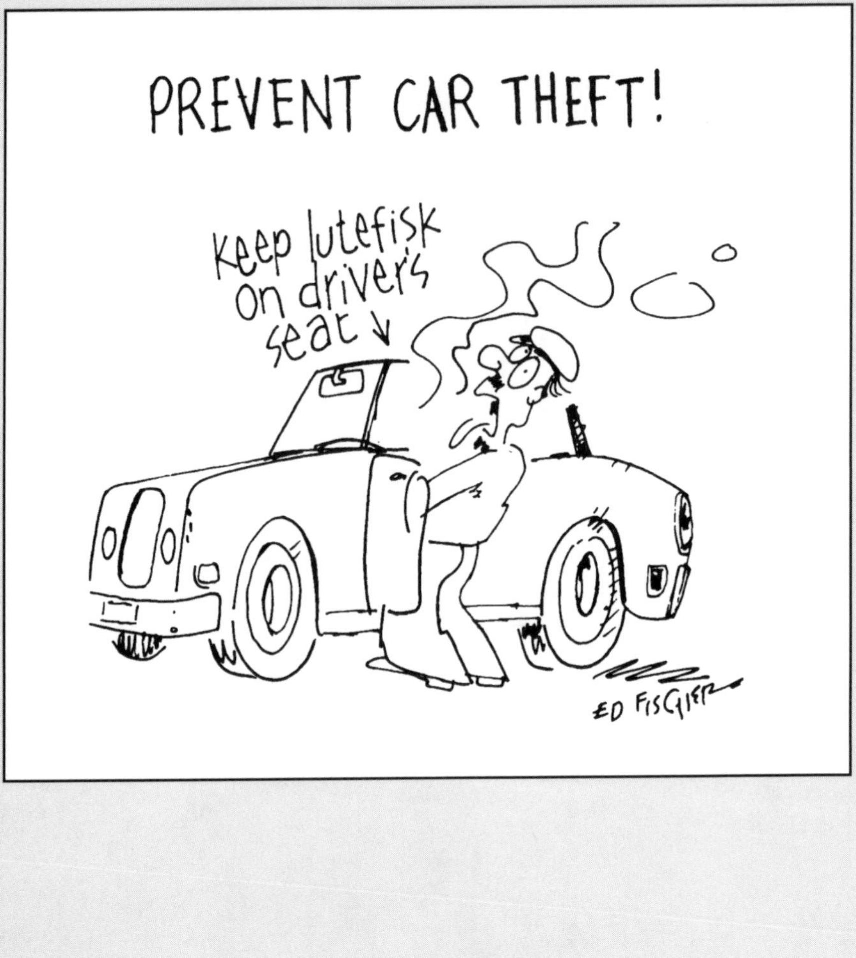
PREVENT CAR THEFT!
Keep lutefisk on driver's seat
ED FISCHER

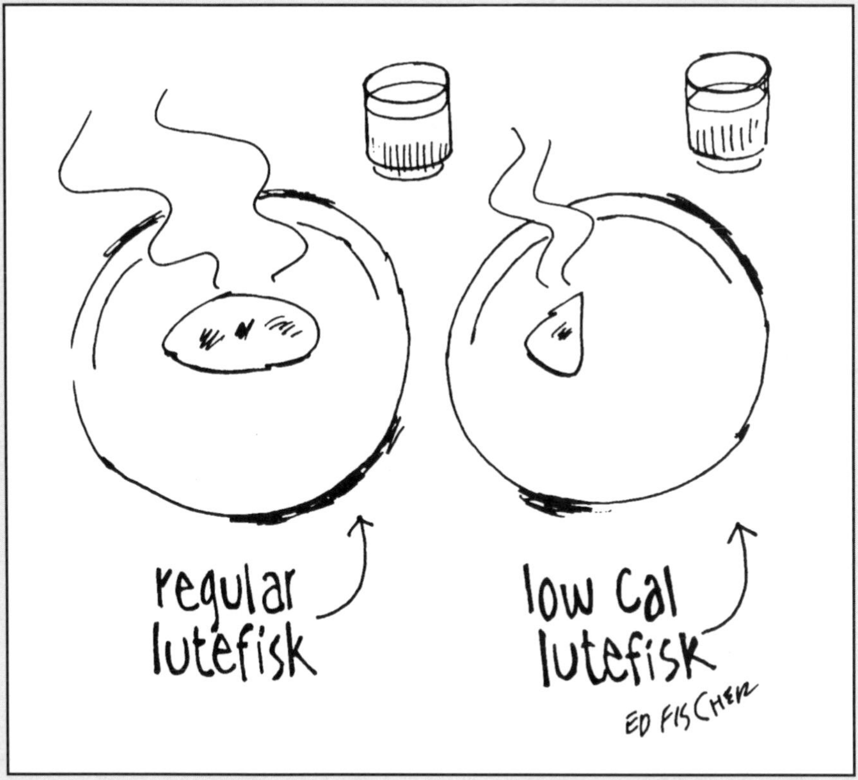
regular lutefisk
low cal lutefisk
ED FISCHER

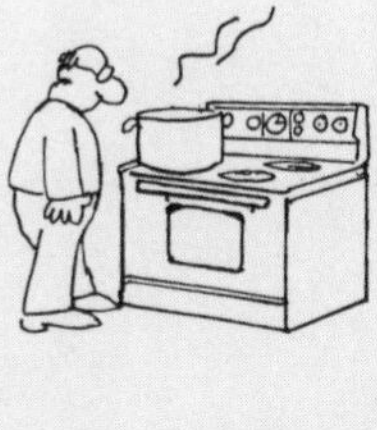

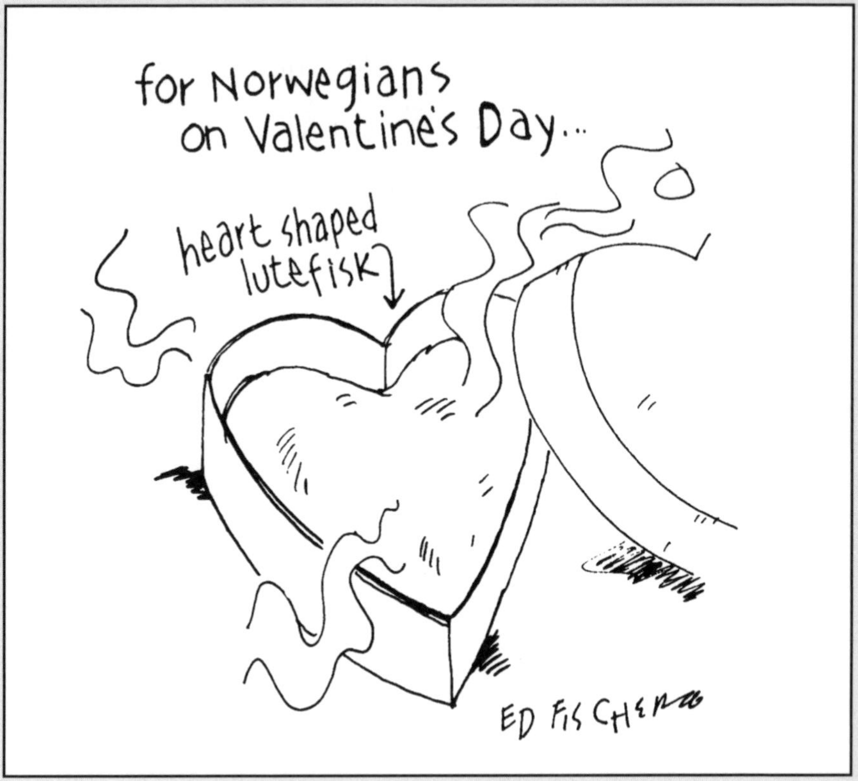

for Norwegians on Valentine's Day...
heart shaped lutefisk
ED FISCHER

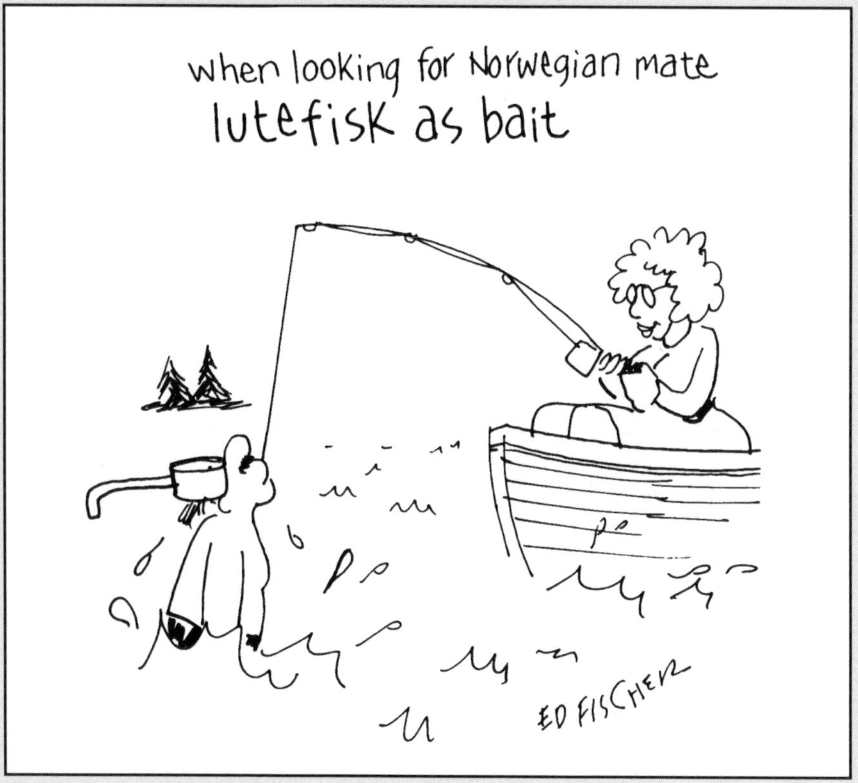
when looking for Norwegian mate
lutefisk as bait
ED FISCHER

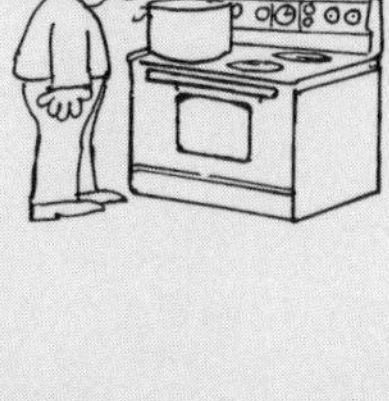

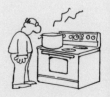

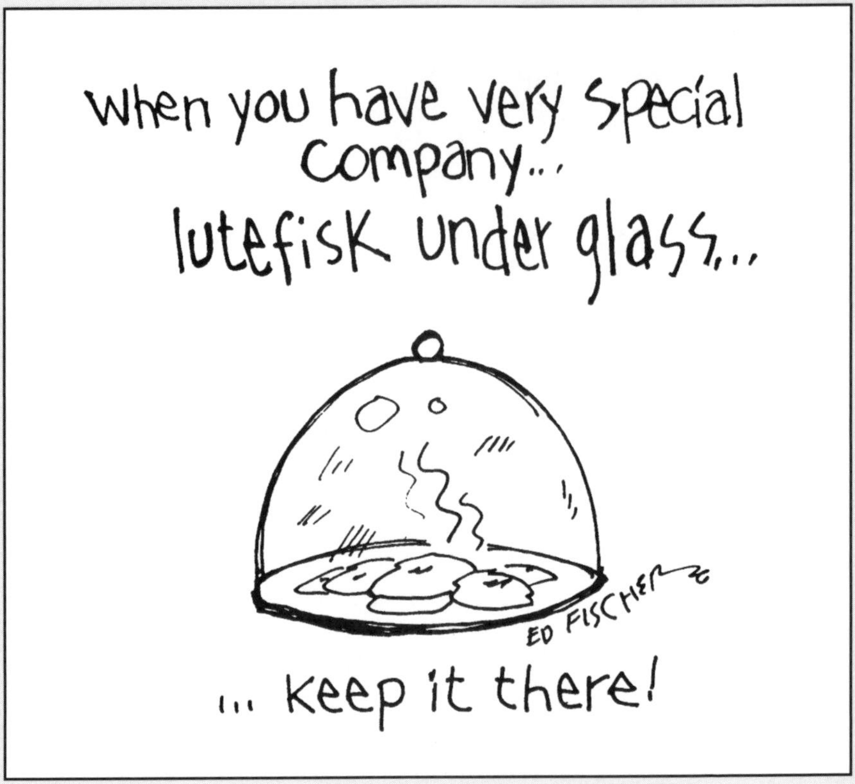
When you have very special company...
lutefisk under glass...
ED FISCHER
... keep it there!

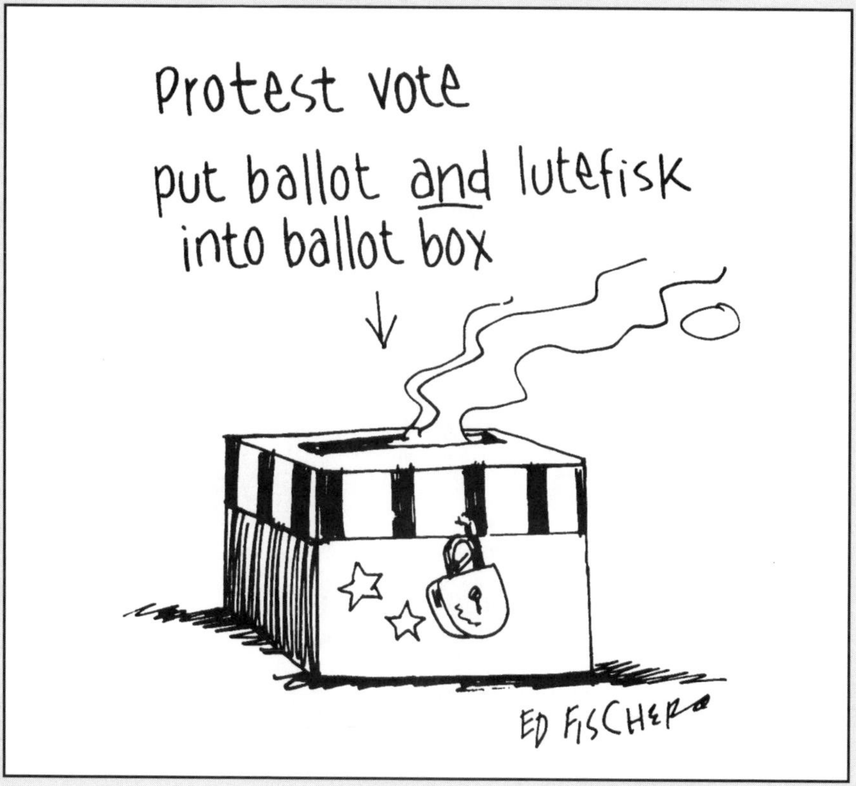
Protest vote
put ballot and lutefisk
into ballot box
ED FISCHER

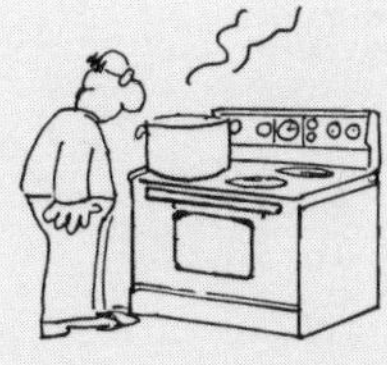

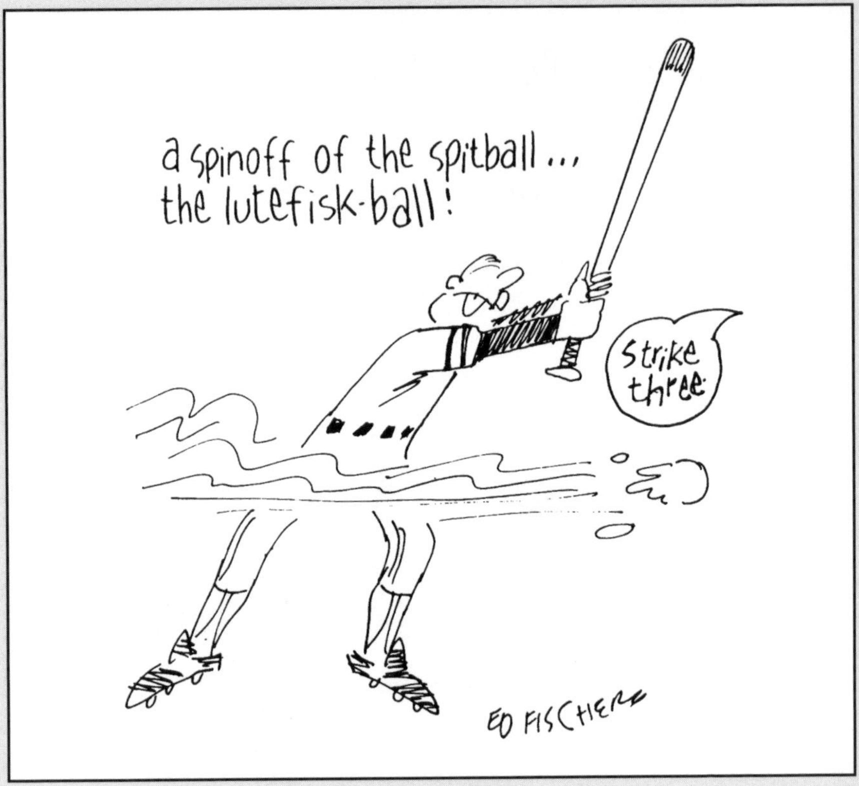
a spinoff of the spitball...
the lutefisk-ball!
Strike three
ED FISCHER

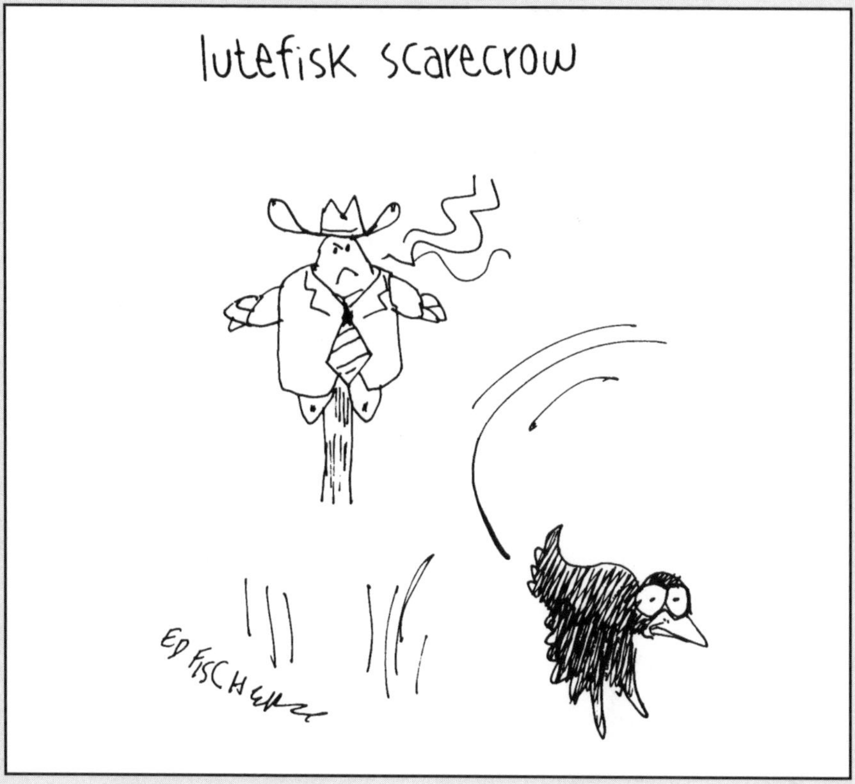
lutefisk scarecrow
ED FISCHER

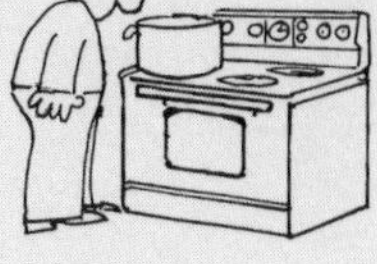

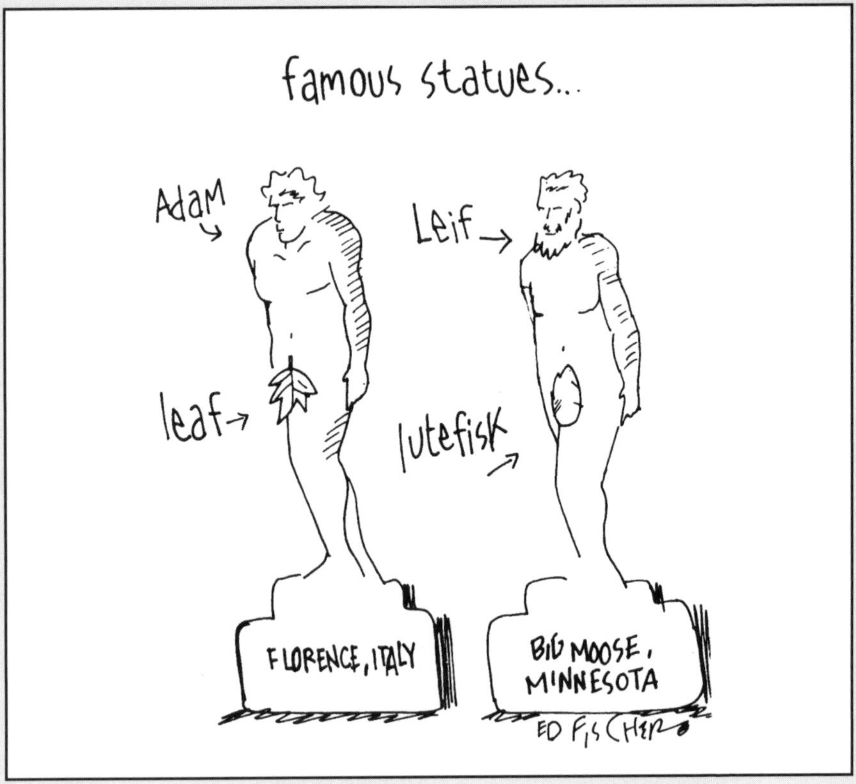
famous statues...
Adam
leaf
FLORENCE, ITALY
Leif
lutefisk
BIG MOOSE, MINNESOTA
ED FISCHER

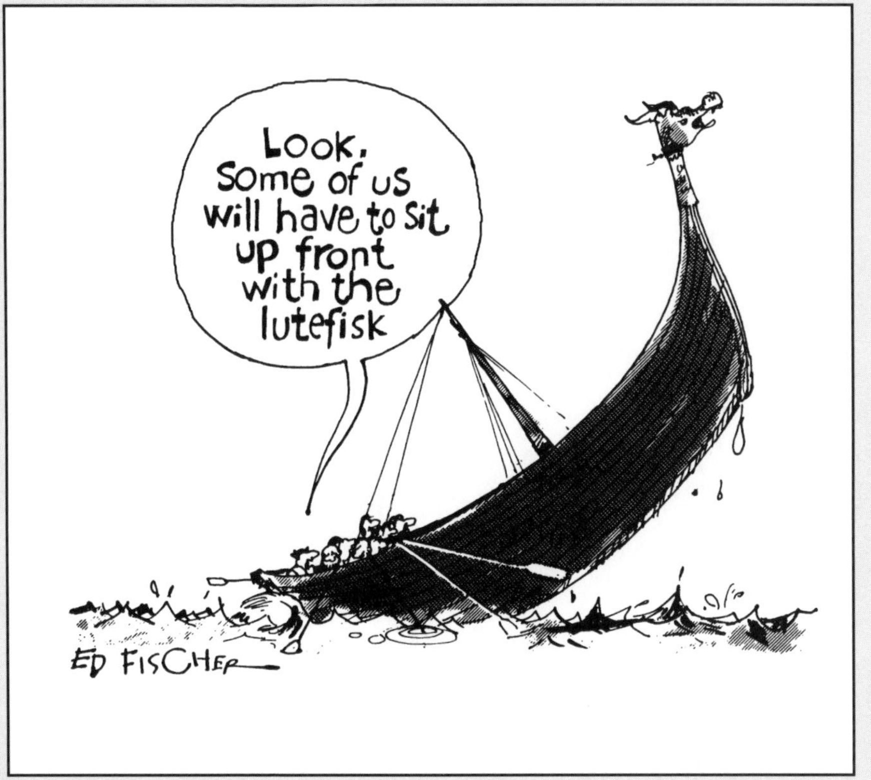
Look, some of us will have to sit up front with the lutefisk
ED FISCHER

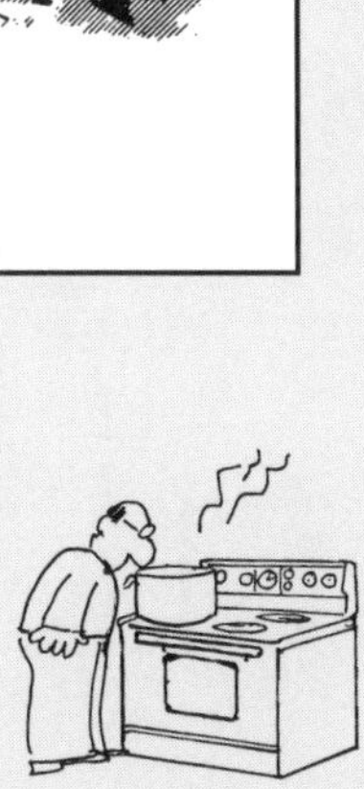

Weird fact: A Scandinavian tribe in northern Norway once used lutefisk for money. They were the most frugal people ever known to man.

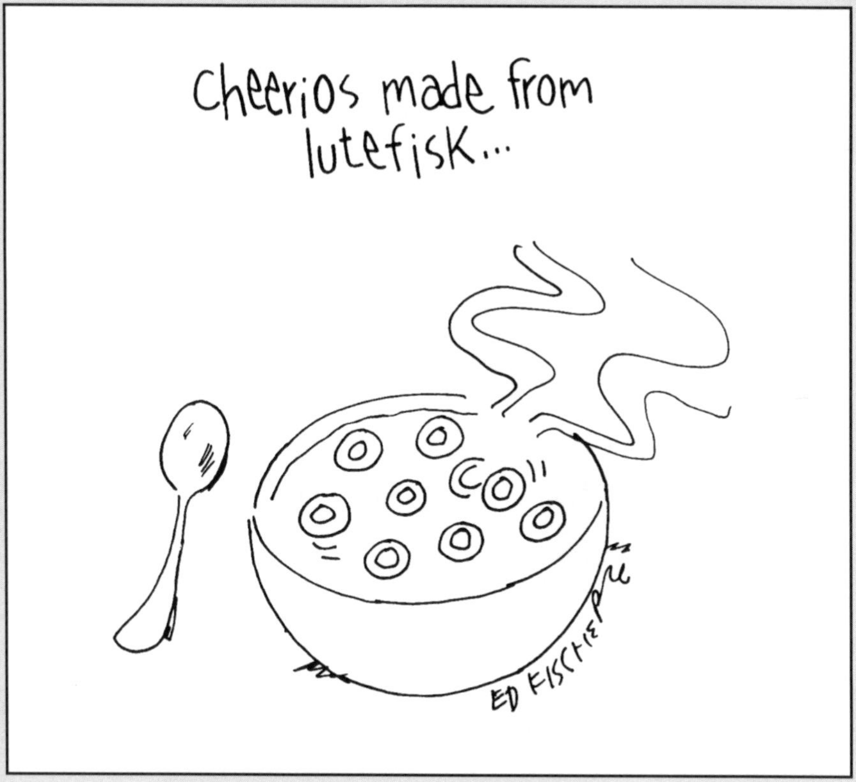
Cheerios made from
lutefisk...
ED FISCHER

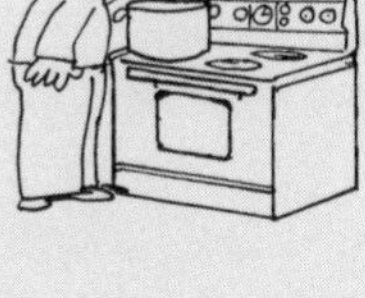

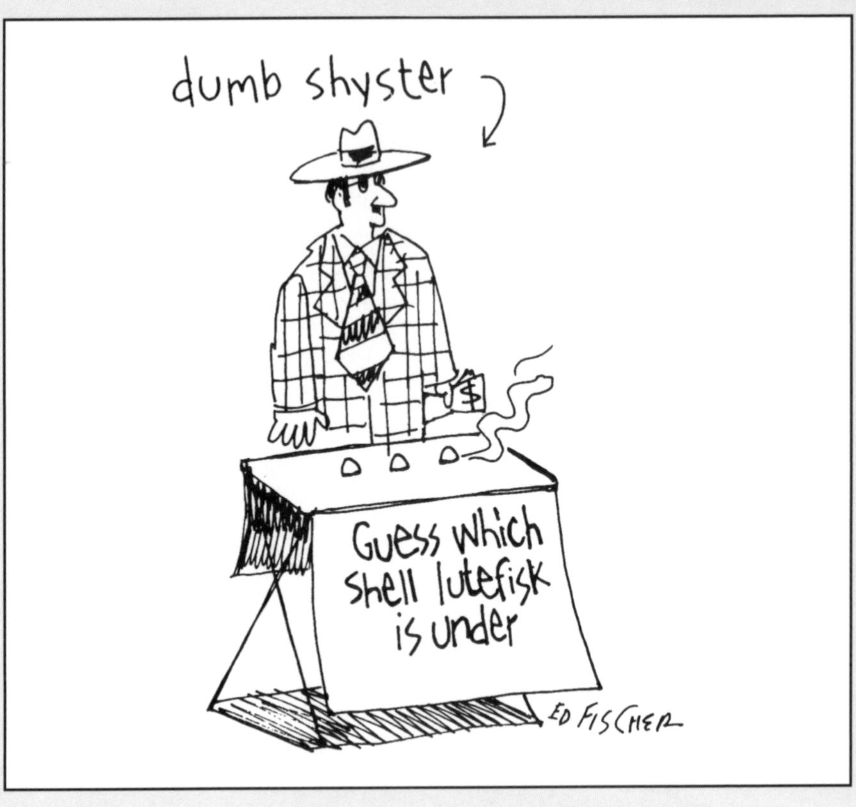
dumb shyster
Guess which shell lutefisk is under
ED FISCHER

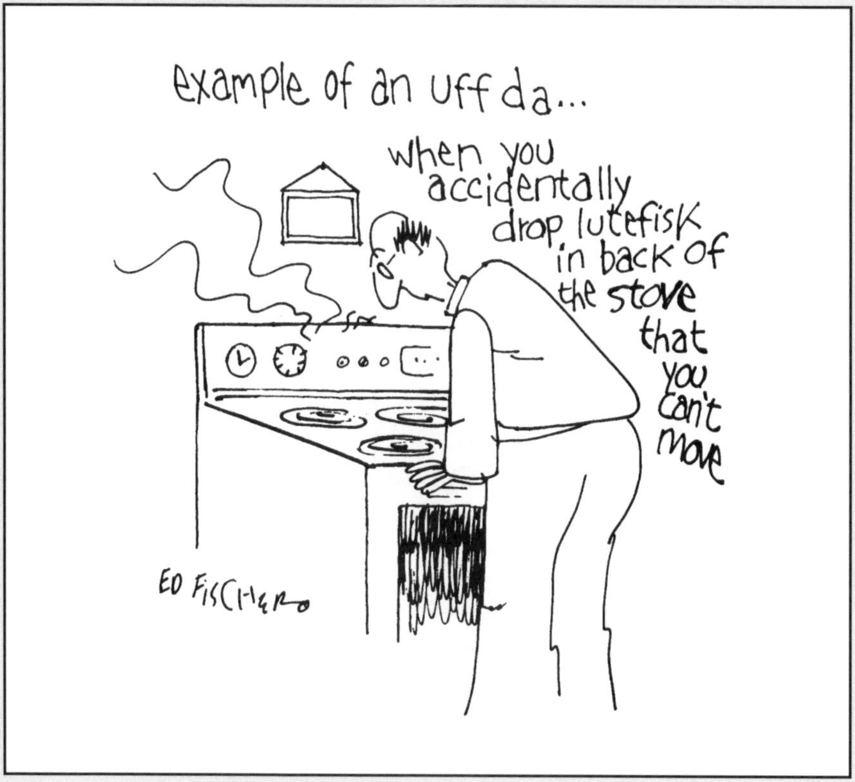
example of an uff da...
when you accidentally drop lutefisk in back of the stove that you can't move
ED FISCHER

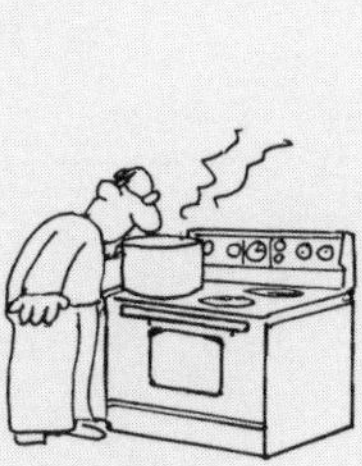

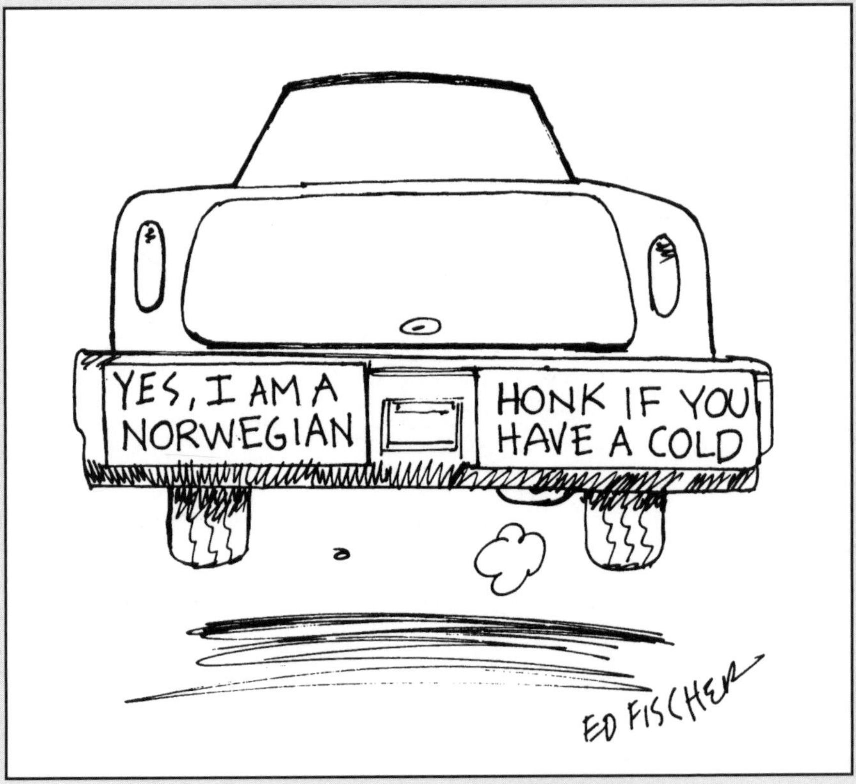
YES, I AM A NORWEGIAN
HONK IF YOU HAVE A COLD
ED FISCHER

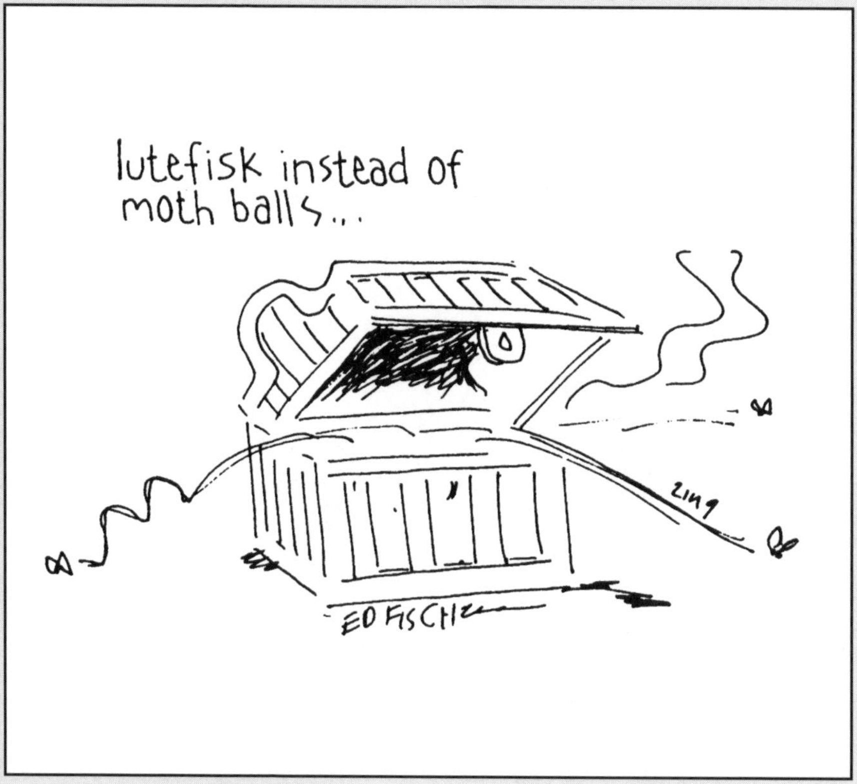
lutefisk instead of
moth balls...
zing
ED FISCHER

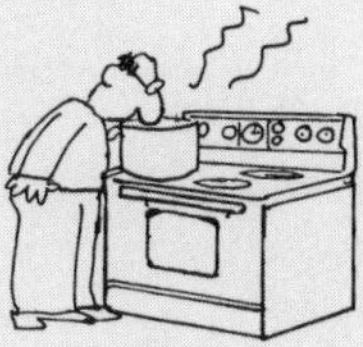

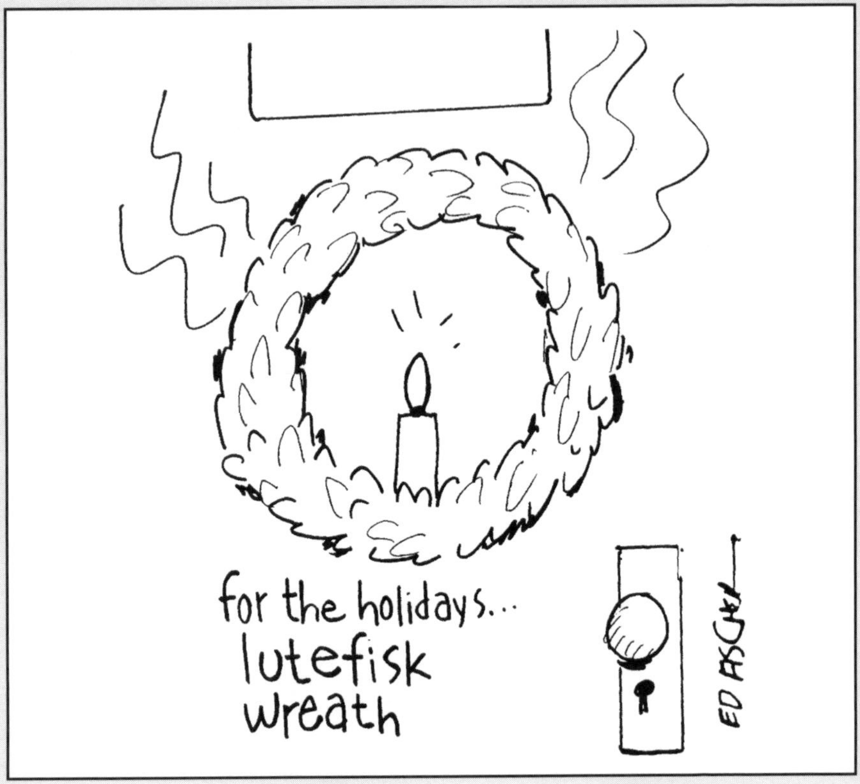
for the holidays...
lutefisk
wreath

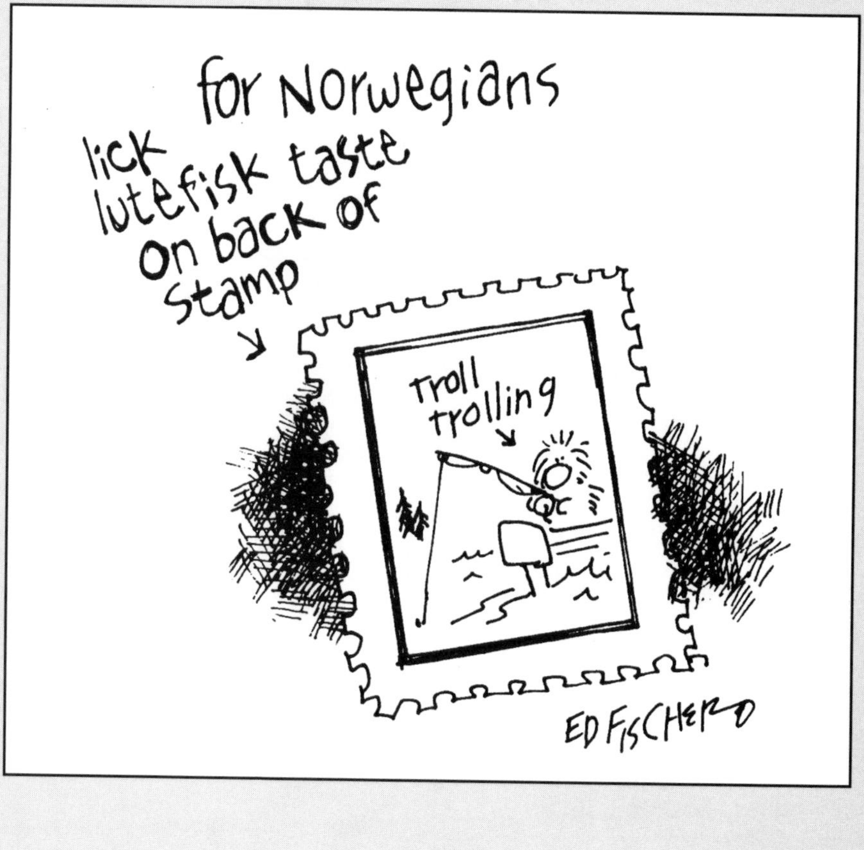
for Norwegians
lick
lutefisk taste
on back of
stamp
Troll
trolling
ED FISCHER

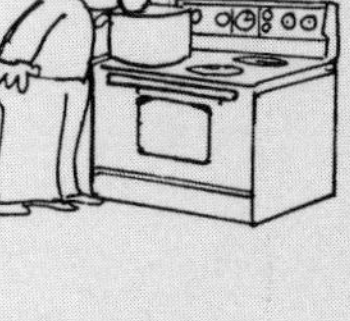

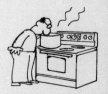

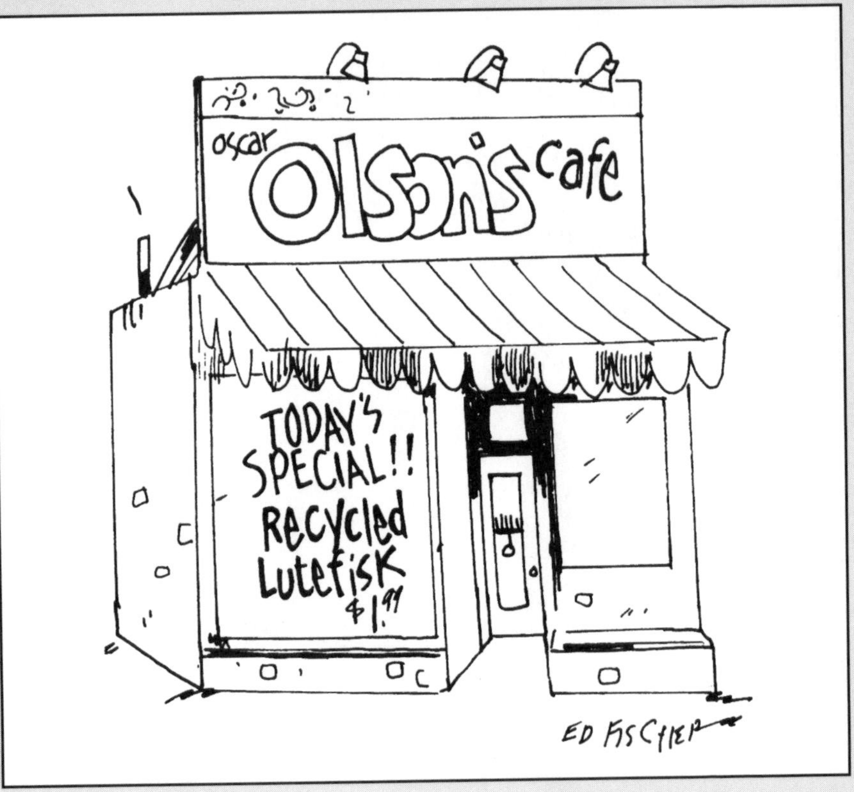
oscar Olson's cafe
TODAY'S SPECIAL!! Recycled Lutefisk $1.99
ED FISCHER

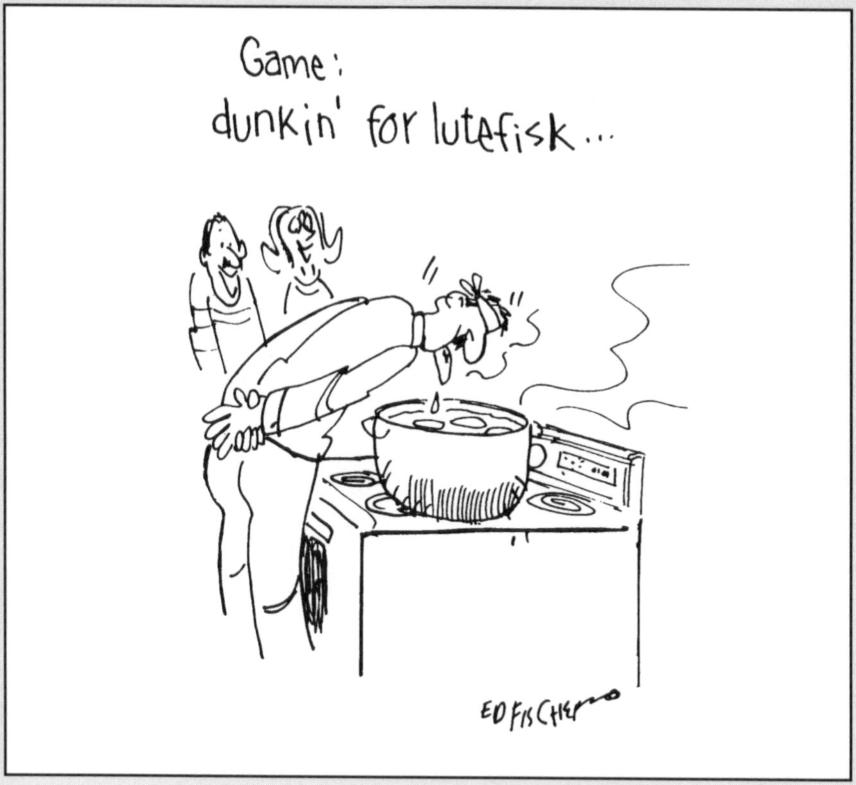
Game:
dunkin' for lutefisk...
ED FISCHER

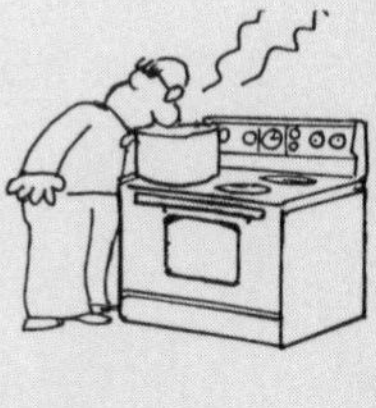

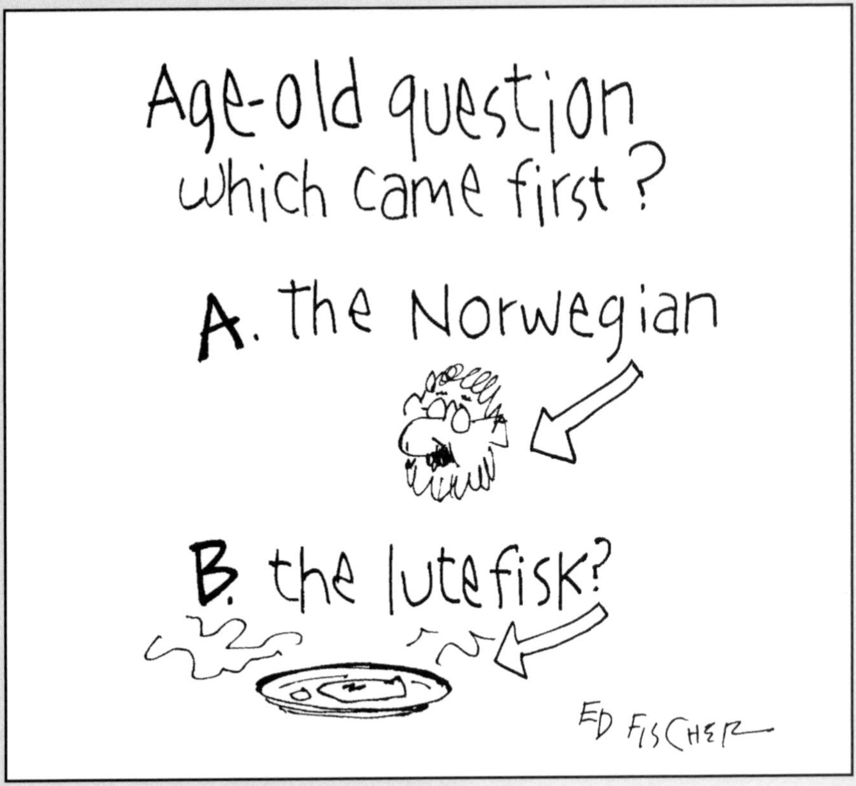
Age-old question
which came first?
A. the Norwegian
B. the lutefisk?
ED FISCHER

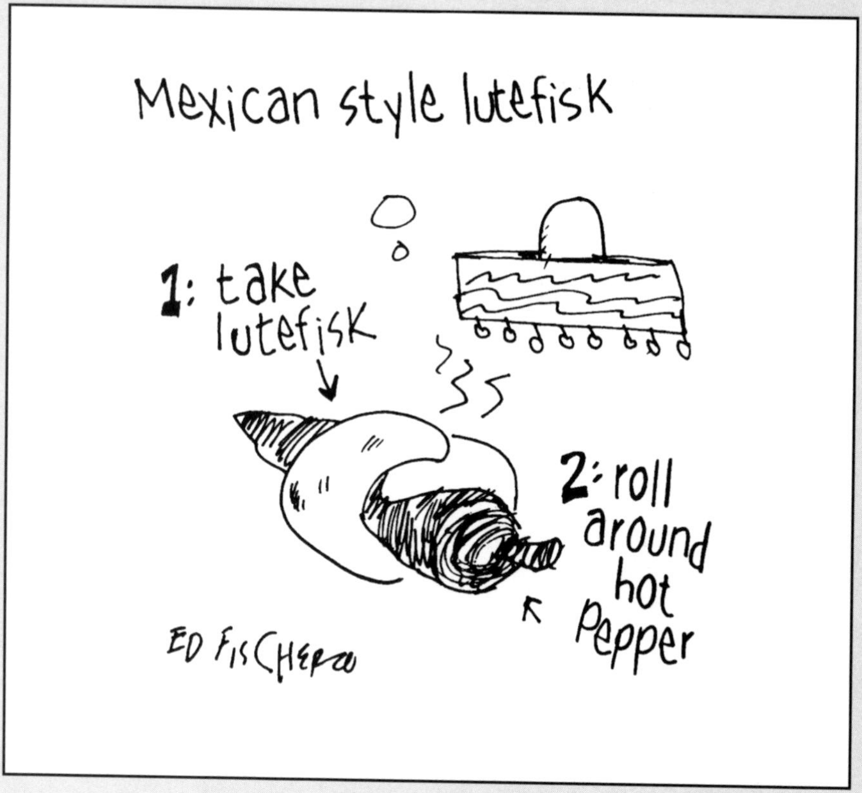
Mexican style lutefisk
1: take lutefisk
2: roll around hot pepper
ED FISCHER

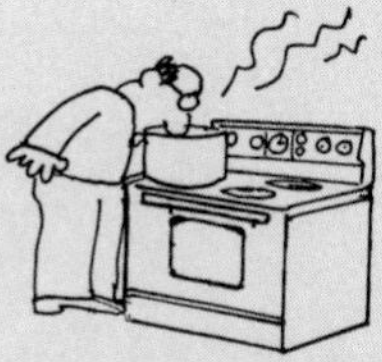

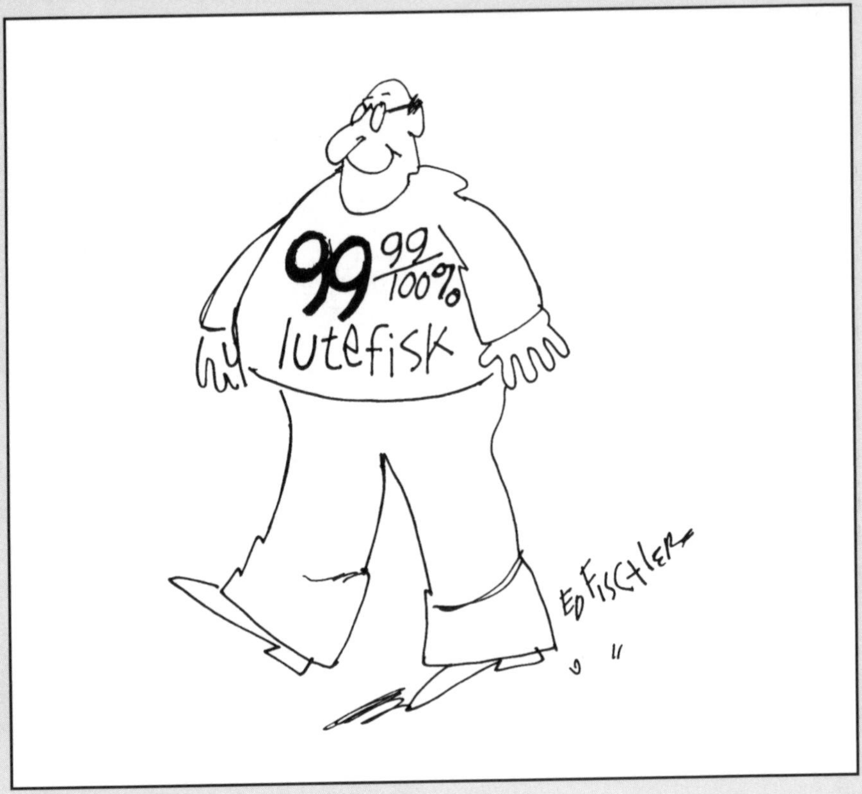
99 99/100%
lutefisk
ED FISCHER

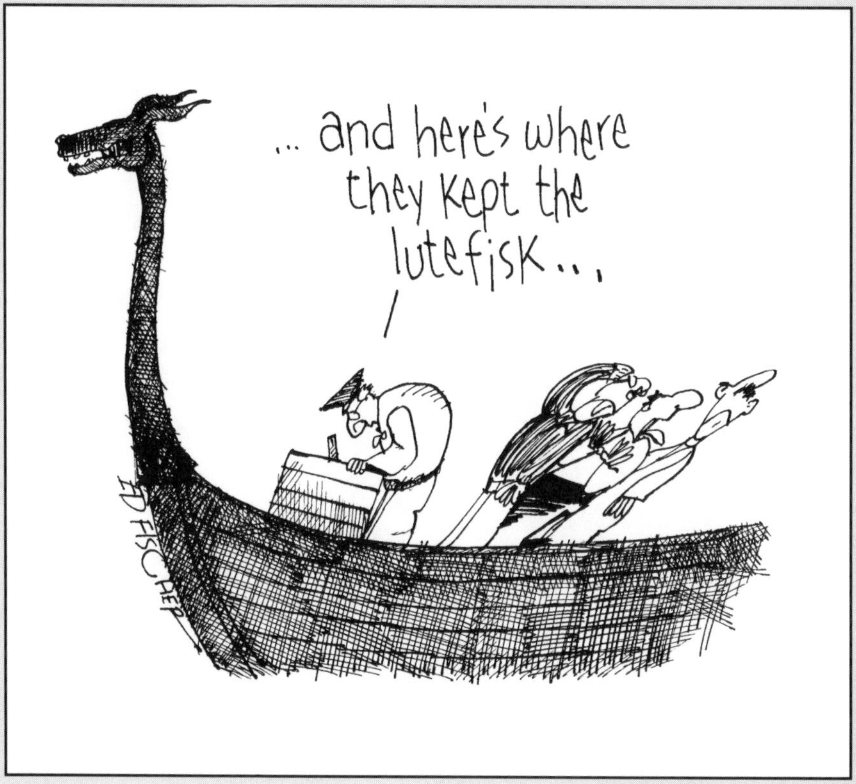
... and here's where they kept the lutefisk...,
ED FISCHER

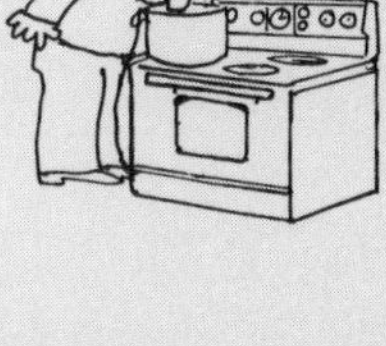

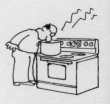

Sven Torgelson of Ollie, Minnesota, says that when his son acts up at a lutefisk meal, he's sent to his room with supper.

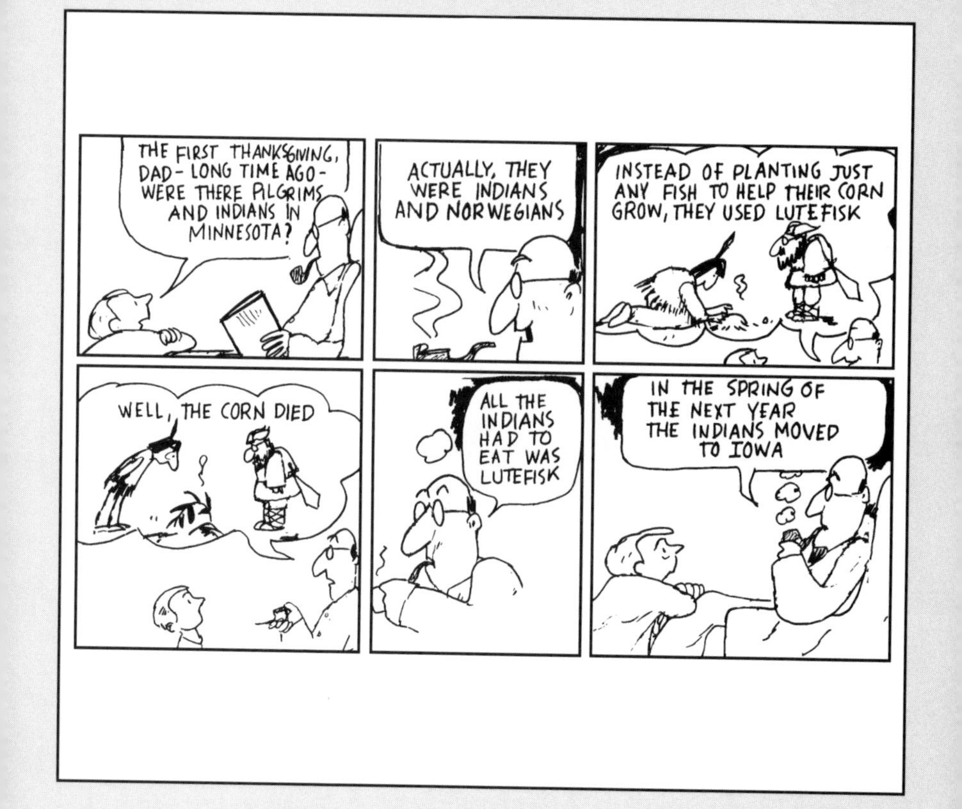
THE FIRST THANKSGIVING, DAD - LONG TIME AGO - WERE THERE PILGRIMS AND INDIANS IN MINNESOTA?
ACTUALLY, THEY WERE INDIANS AND NORWEGIANS
INSTEAD OF PLANTING JUST ANY FISH TO HELP THEIR CORN GROW, THEY USED LUTEFISK
WELL, THE CORN DIED
ALL THE INDIANS HAD TO EAT WAS LUTEFISK
IN THE SPRING OF THE NEXT YEAR THE INDIANS MOVED TO IOWA

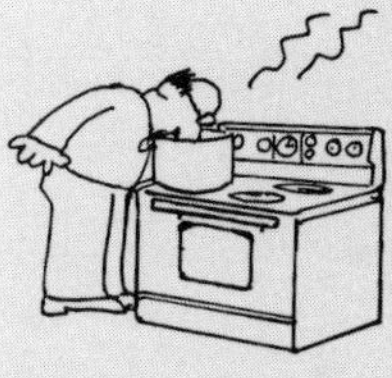

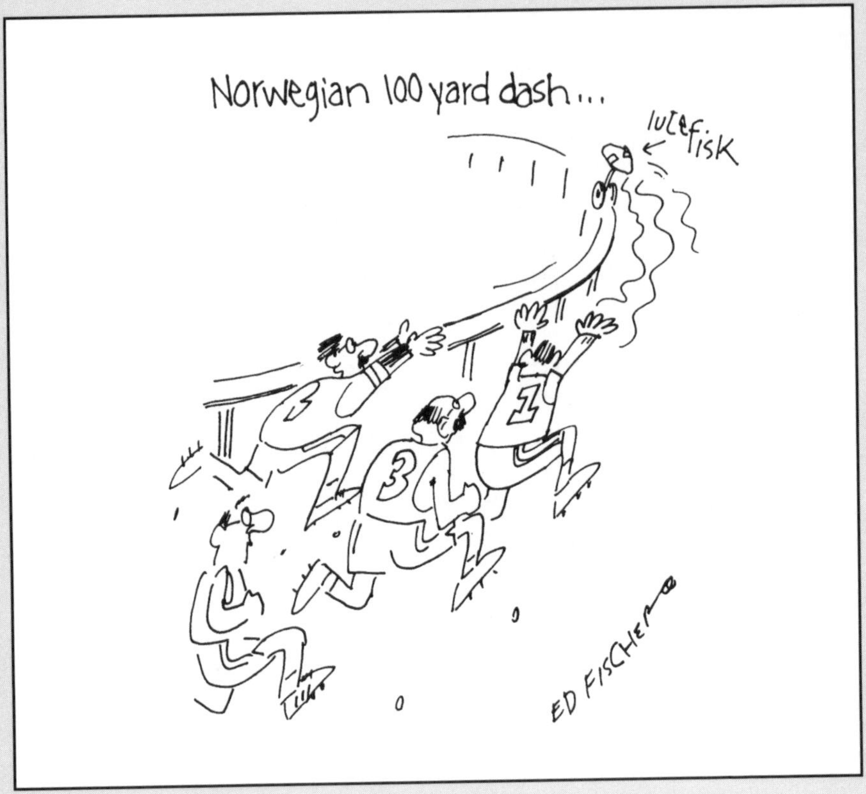
Norwegian 100 yard dash...
lutefisk
1
3
ED FISCHER

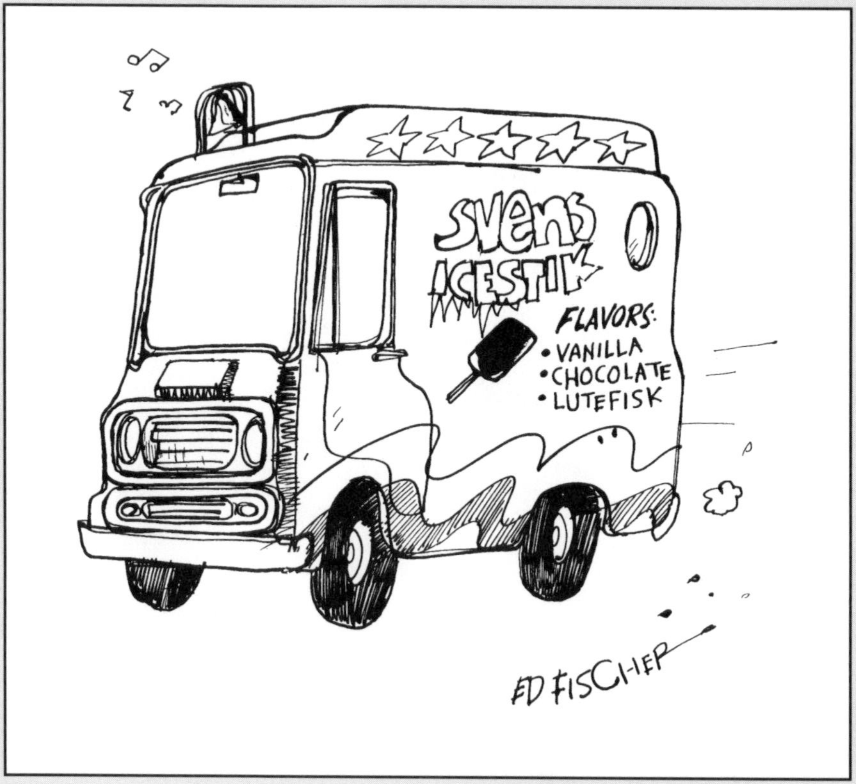
SVENS
ICESTIK
FLAVORS:
• VANILLA
• CHOCOLATE
• LUTEFISK
ED FISCHER

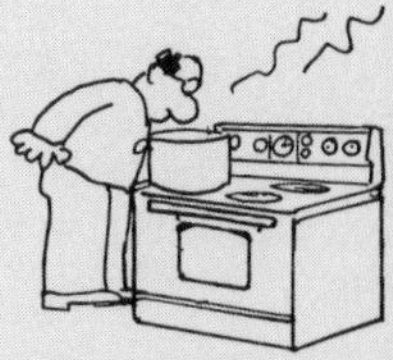

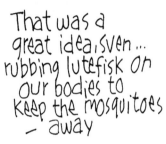

That was a great idea, Sven... rubbing lutefisk on our bodies to keep the mosquitoes — away

ED FISCHER

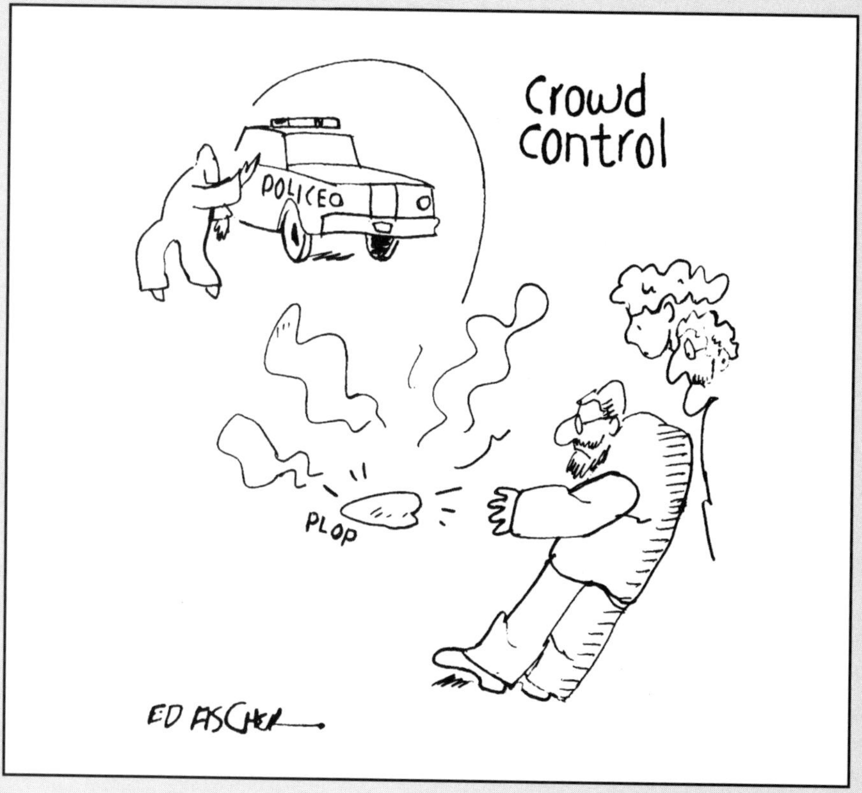
Crowd
control
POLICE
PLOP
ED FISCHER

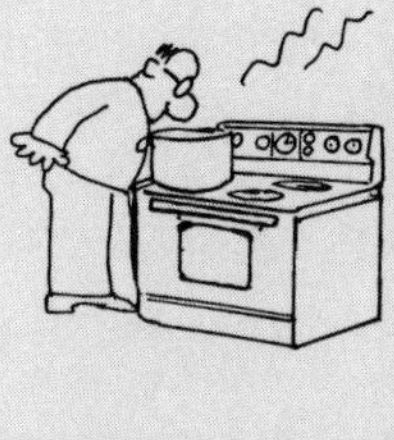

Dale of Duck, Wisconsin, tells this joke: Few people know about Charlie Lindson of Svenborg, Minnesota, who was the very first pilot, even before Lindbergh, to cross the Atlantic from New York to Paris. Unfortunately, his plane carried a large load of lutefisk so nobody met him at the airport.

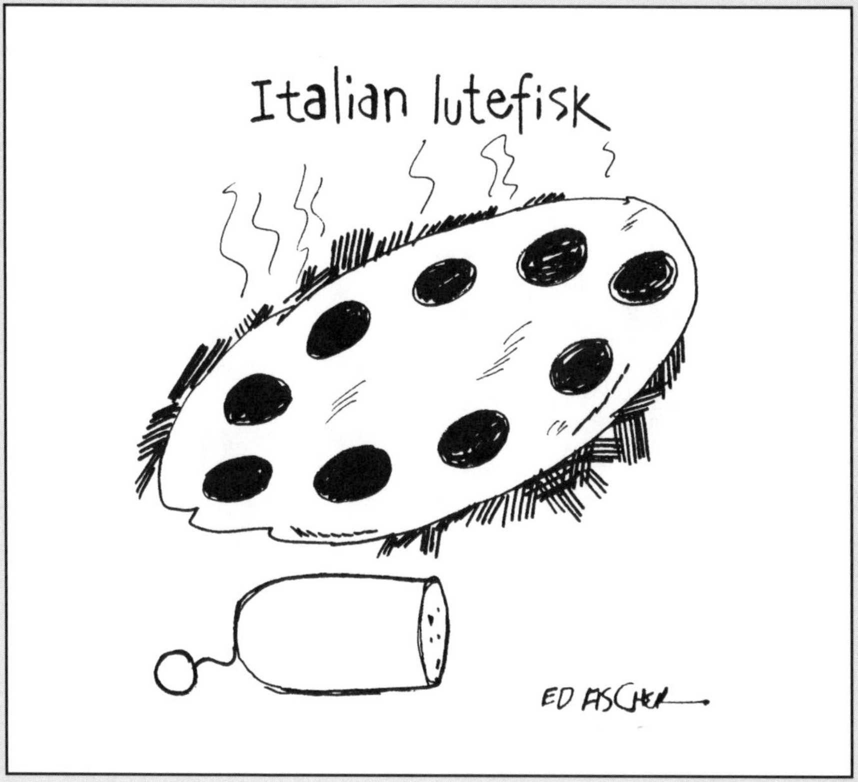
Italian lutefisk
ED FISCHER

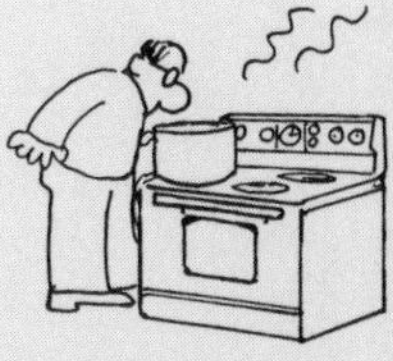

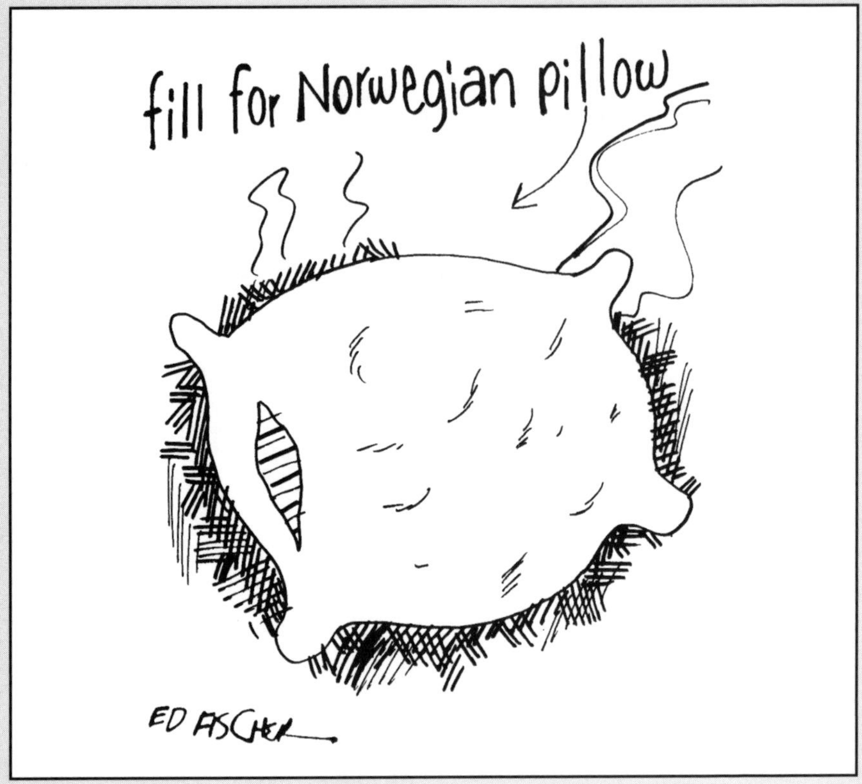
fill for Norwegian pillow
ED FISCHER

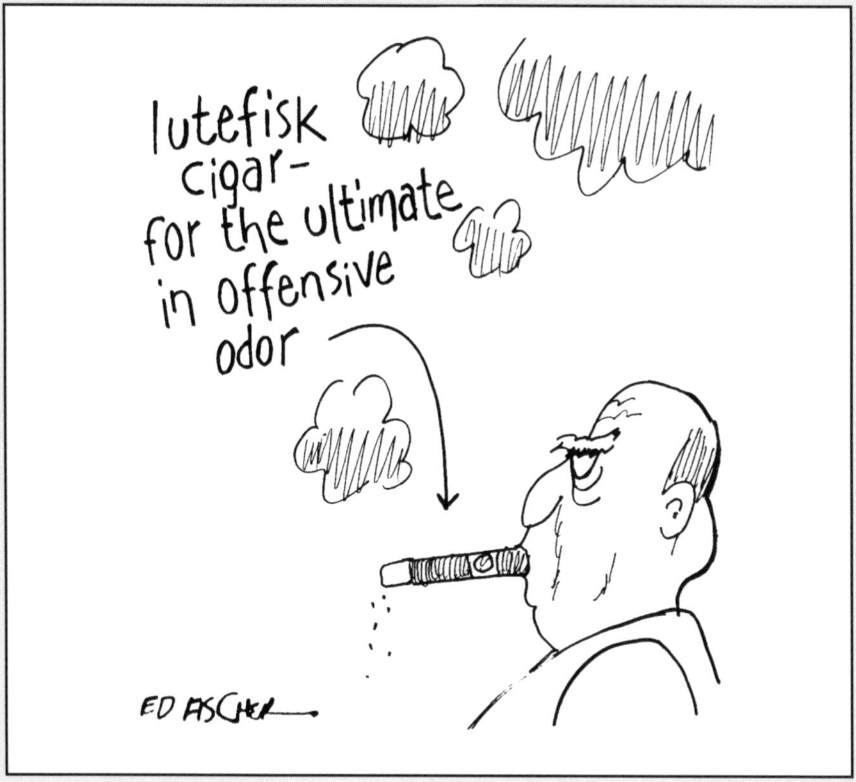
lutefisk
cigar-
for the ultimate
in offensive
odor
ED FISCHER

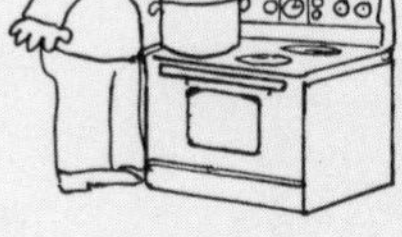

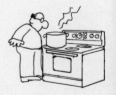

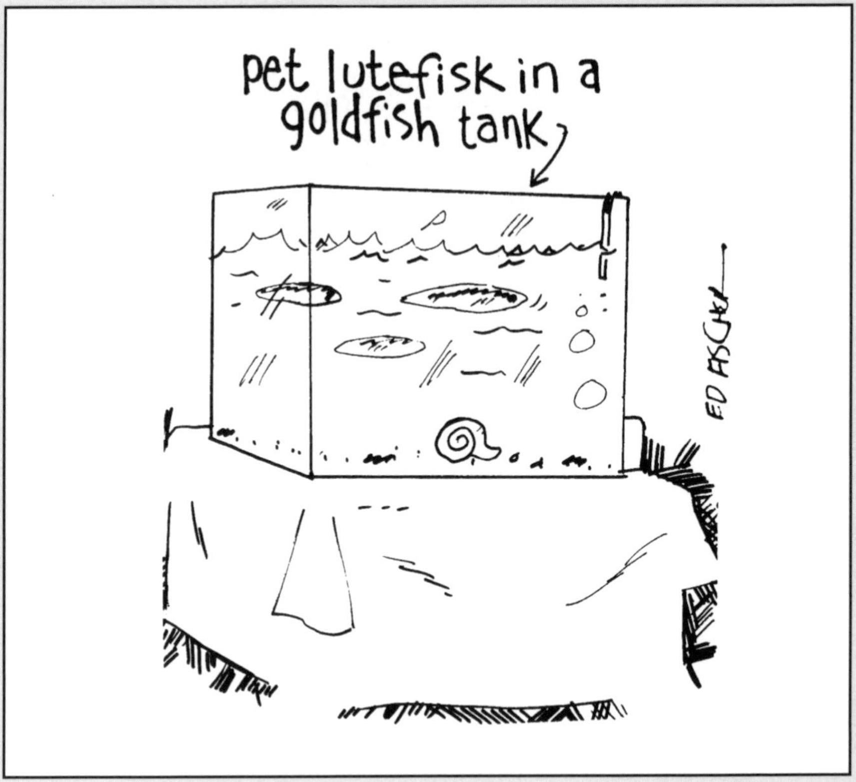
pet lutefisk in a goldfish tank
ED FISCHER

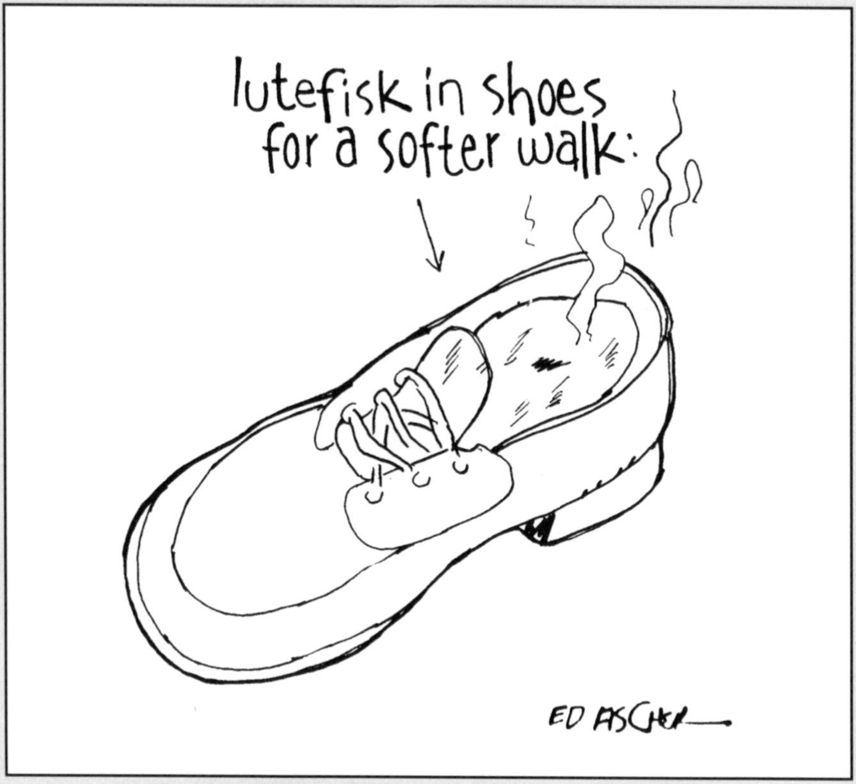
lutefisk in shoes
for a softer walk:
ED FISCHER

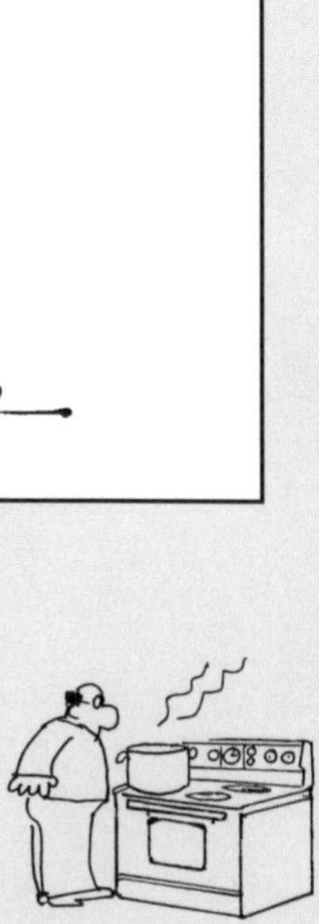

Nels Fuggleson of Roaring Pine City likes to tell this favorite lutefisk story: Oscar goes into a store and asks the clerk for two pounds of lutefisk. The clerk asks, "Are you Norwegian?" "Why in blazes do you ask that?" Oscar fumes. "What makes you think I'm not German or Polish?" "Because," the clerk says, "this is a hardware store."

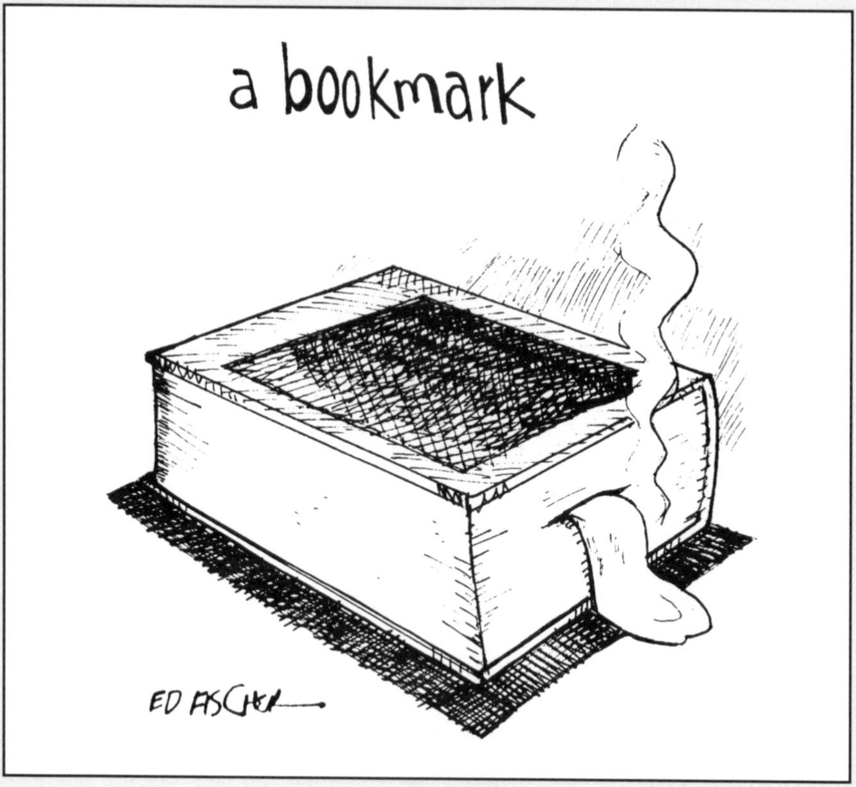
a bookmark
ED FISCHER

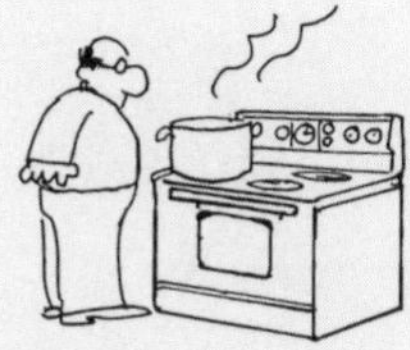

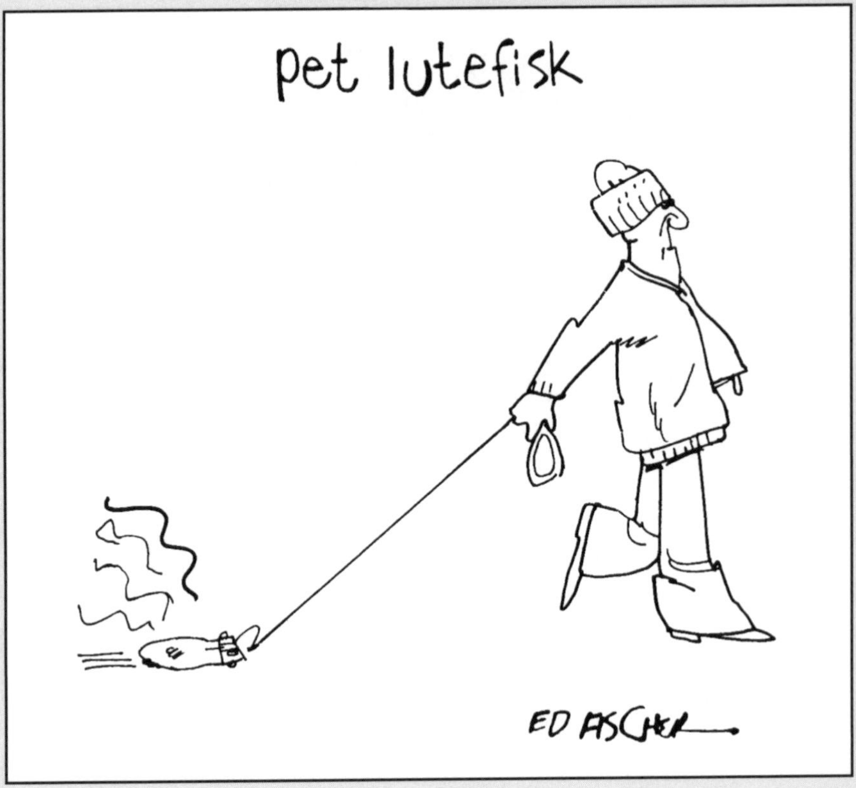
pet lutefisk
ED FISCHER

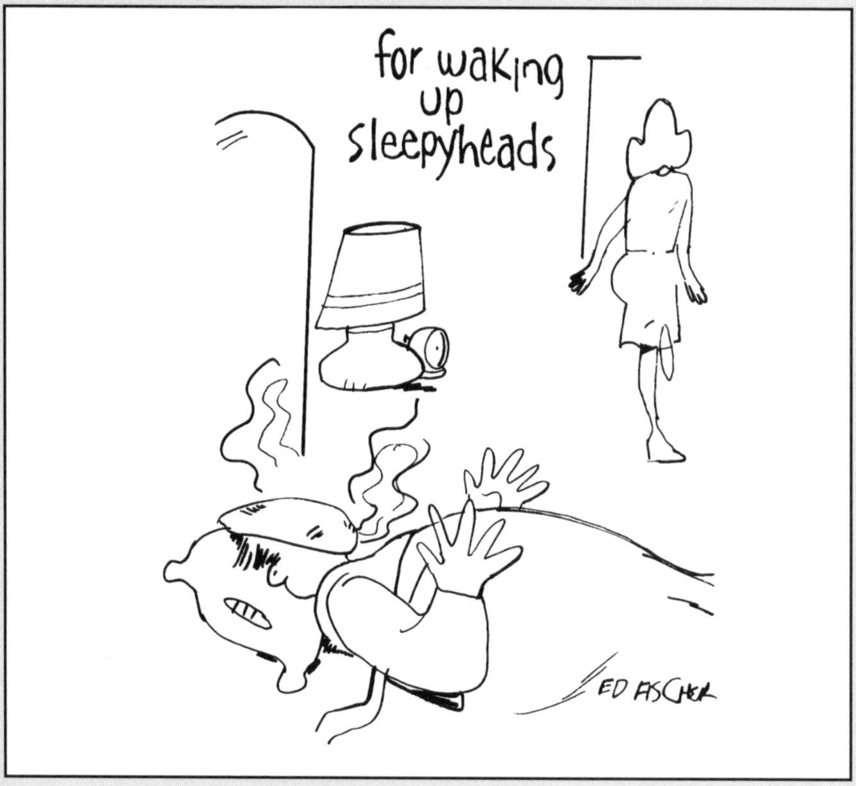
for waking up sleepyheads
ED FISCHER

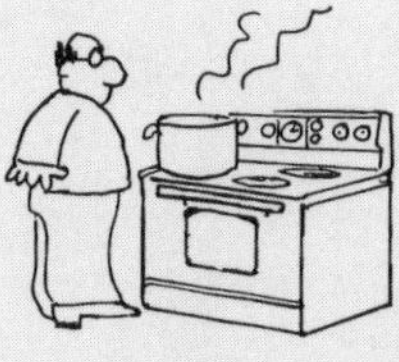

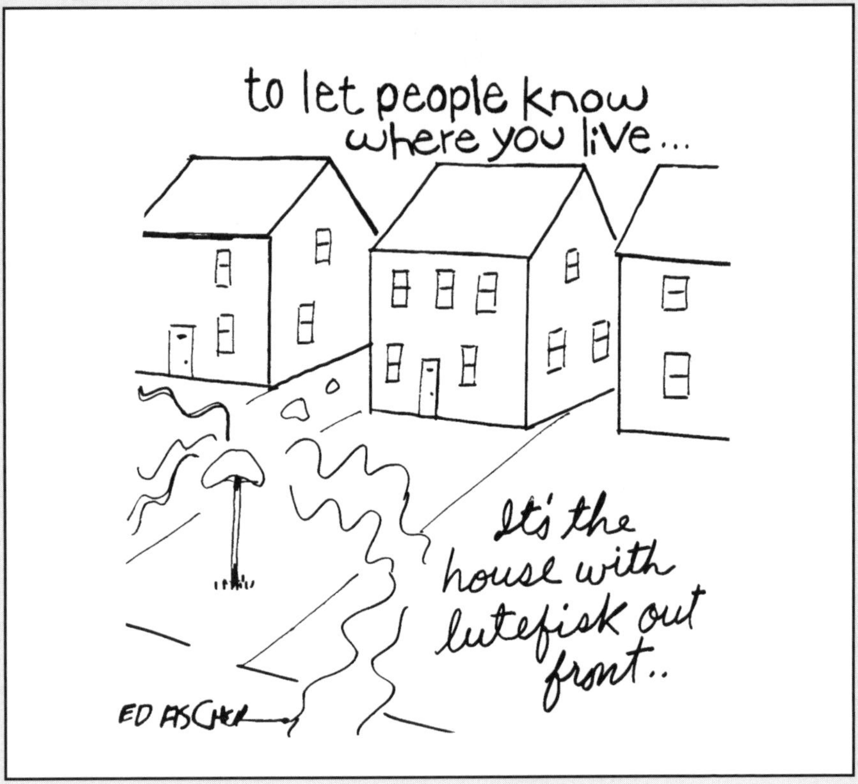
to let people know
where you live...
It's the
house with
lutefisk out
front..
ED FISCHER

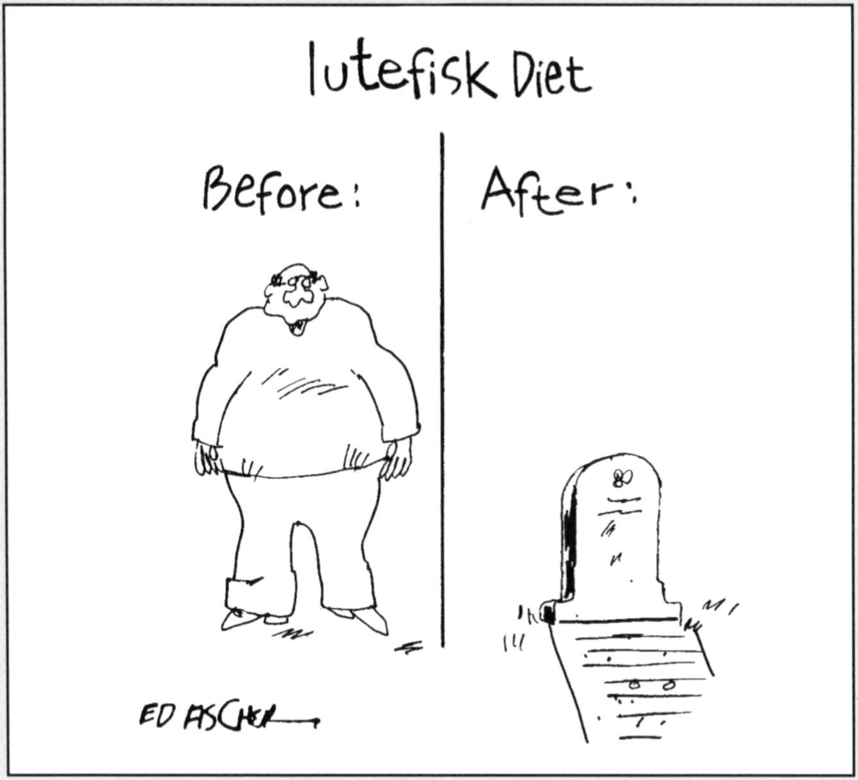
lutefisk Diet
Before:
After:
ED FISCHER

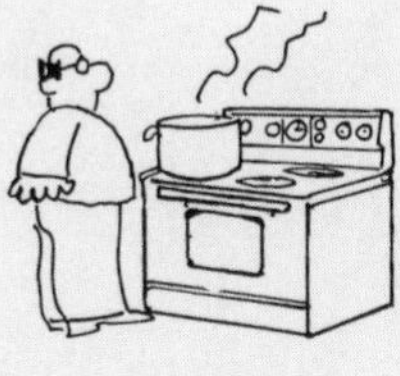

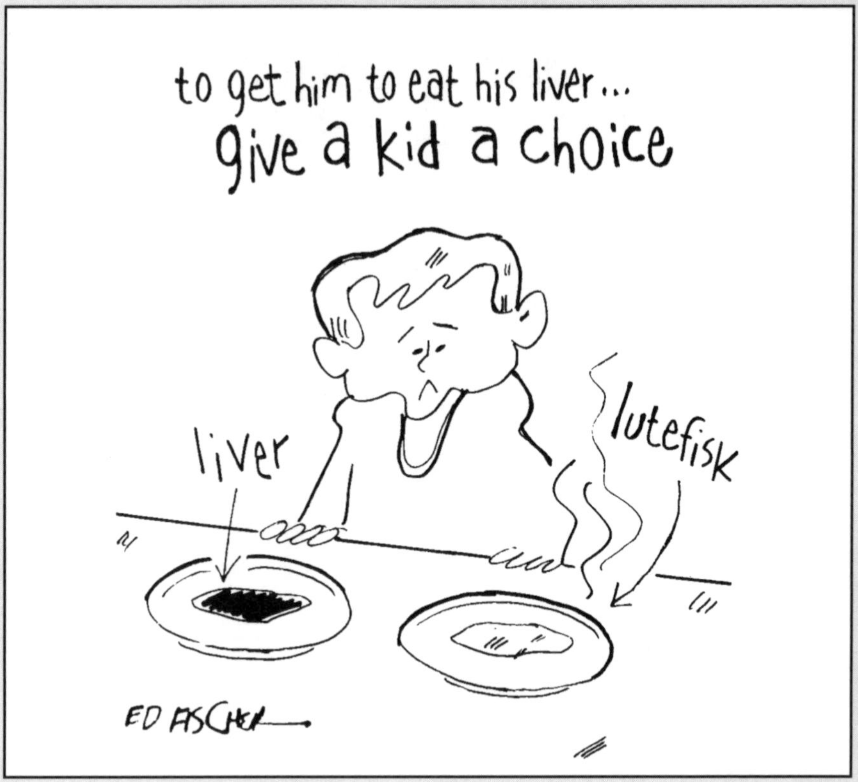
to get him to eat his liver...
give a kid a choice
liver
lutefisk
ED FISCHER

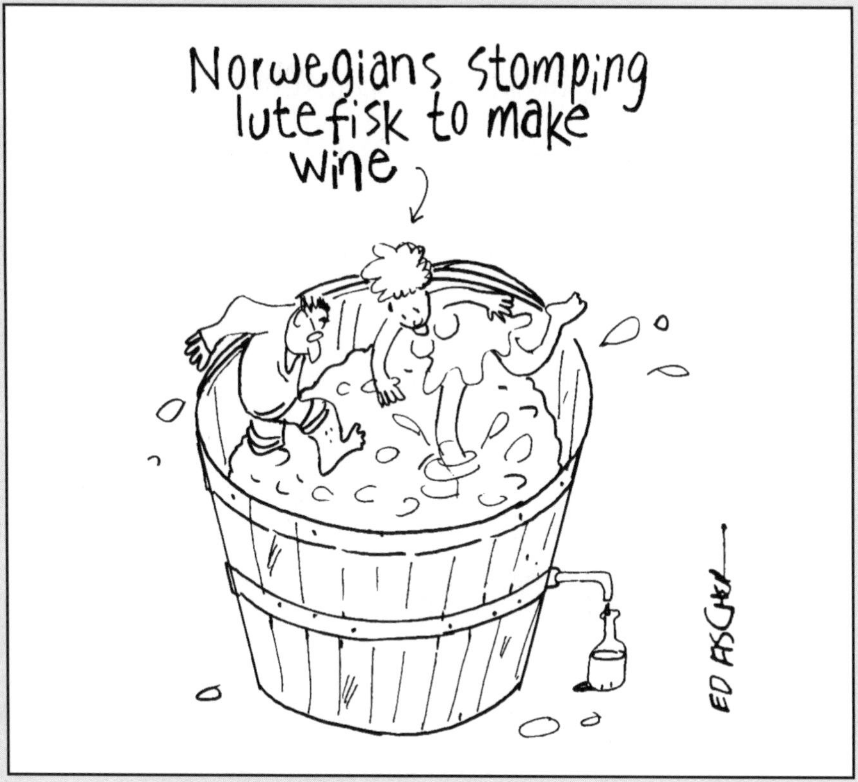
Norwegians stomping lutefisk to make wine
ED FISCHER

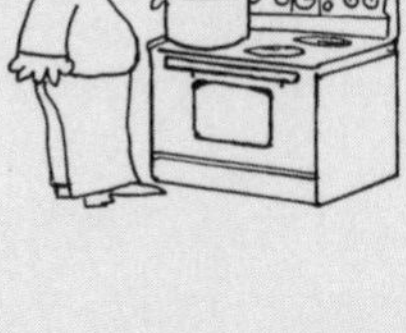

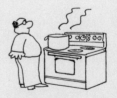

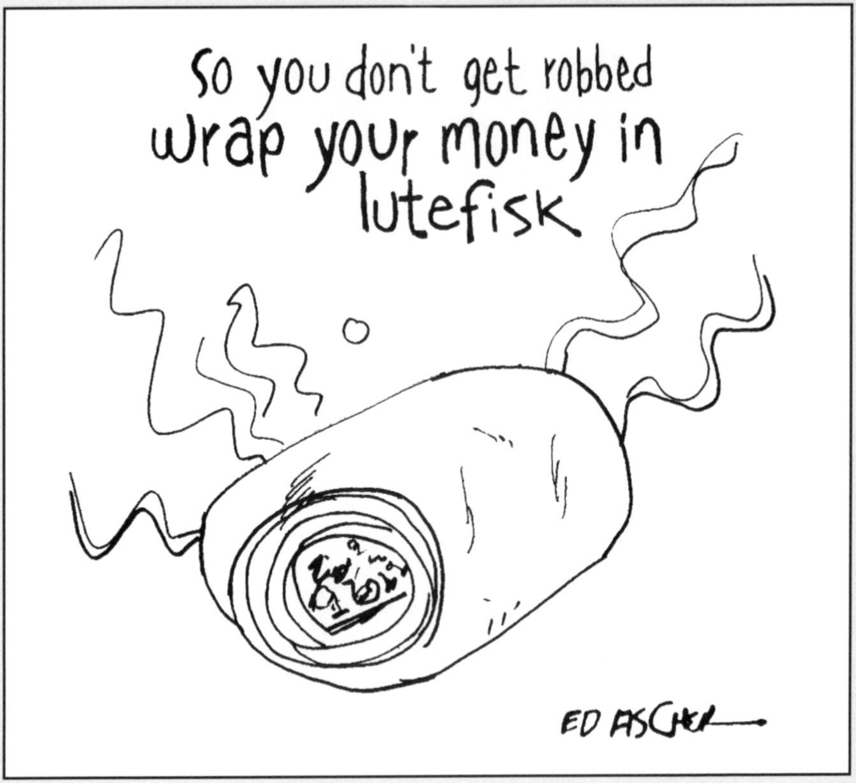
So you don't get robbed
wrap your money in
lutefisk
ED FISCHER

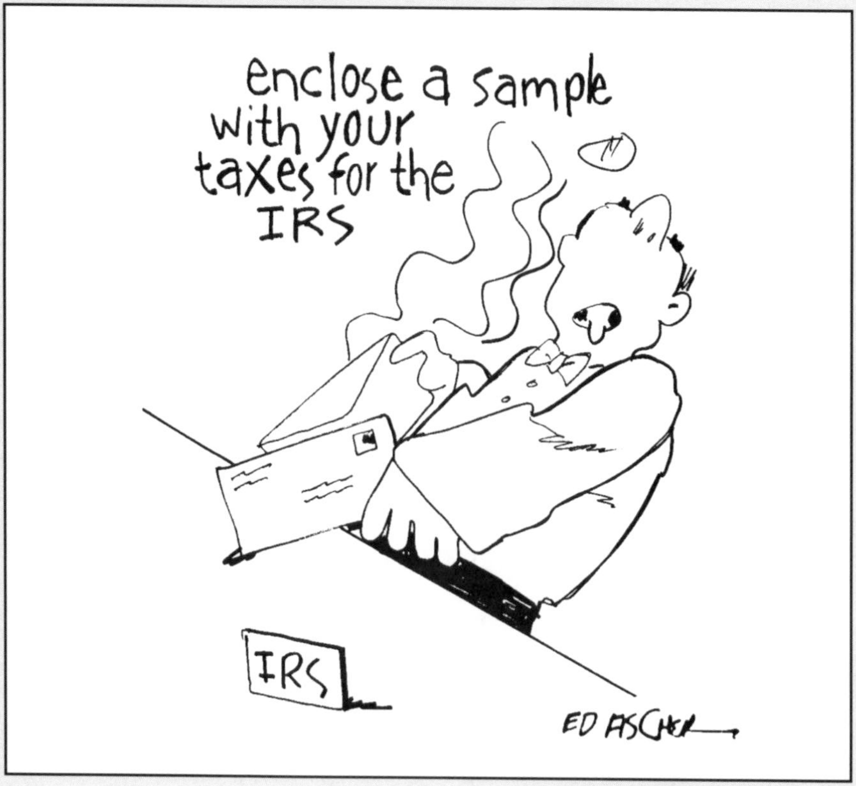
enclose a sample with your taxes for the IRS
IRS
ED FISCHER

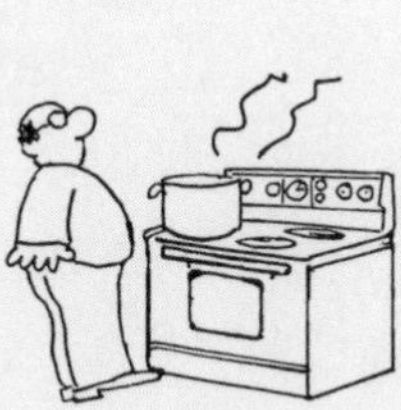

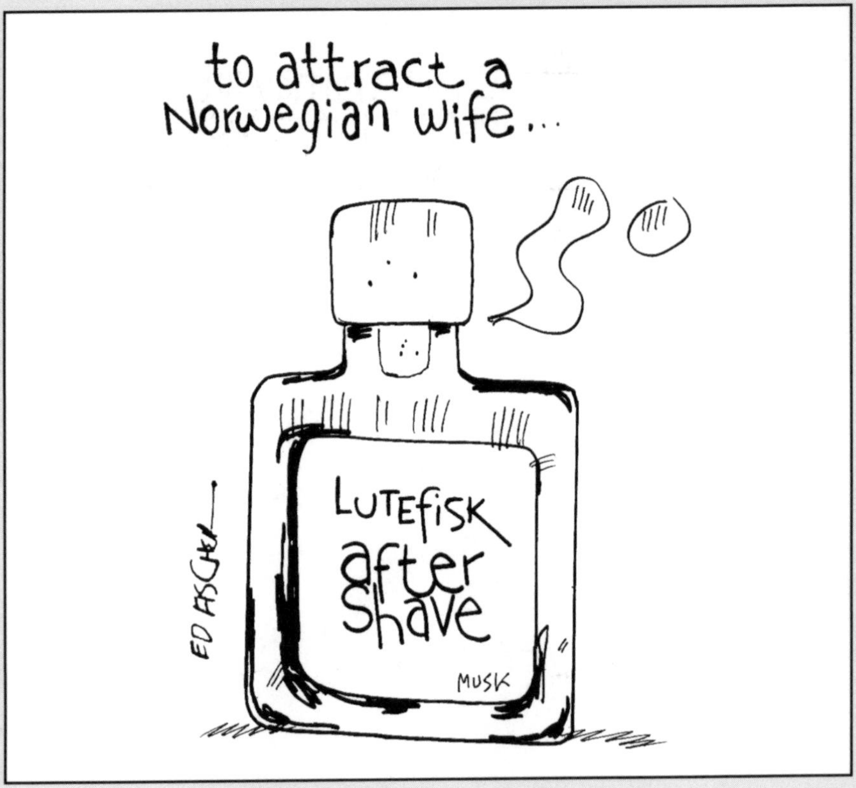
to attract a Norwegian wife...
LUTEfisK
after Shave
MUSK
ED FISCHER

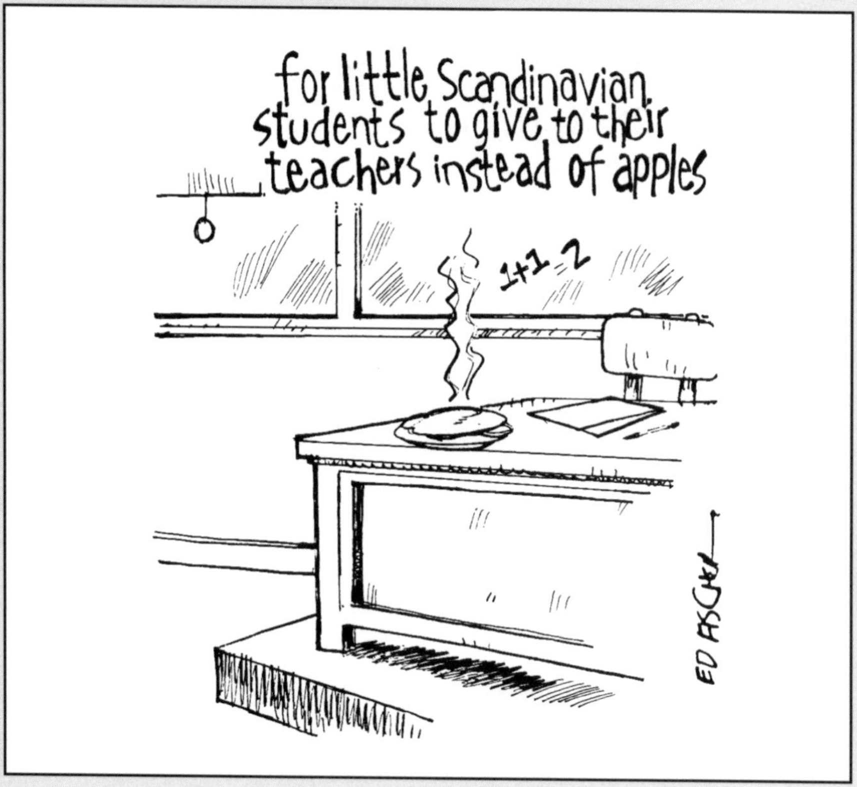
for little Scandinavian students to give to their teachers instead of apples
1+1=2
ED FISCHER

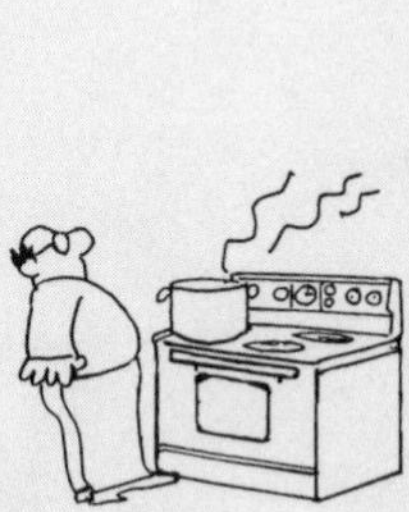

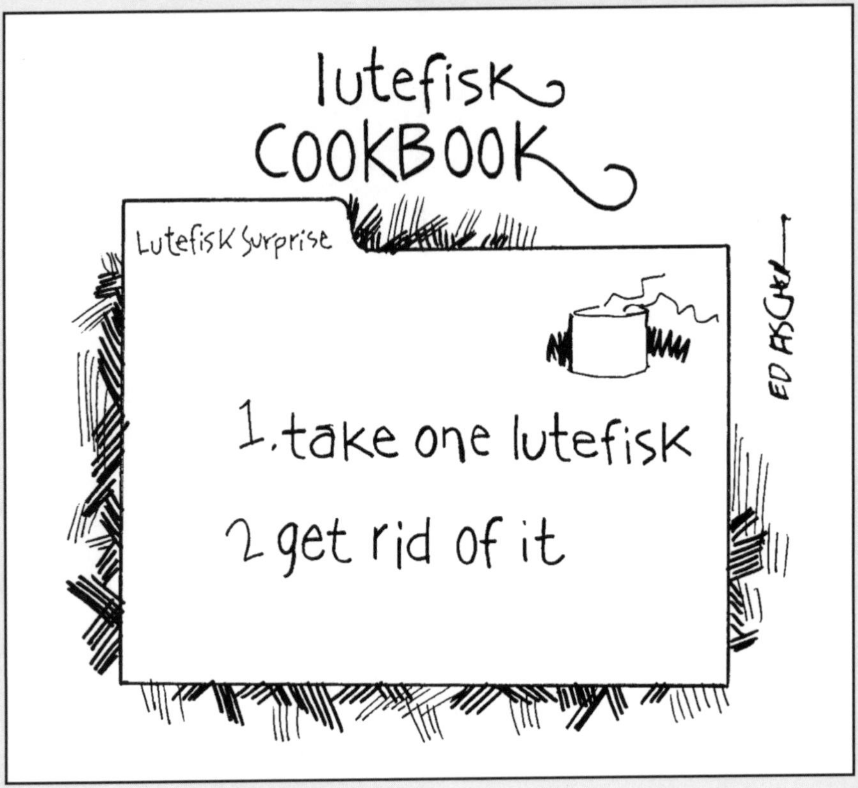
lutefisk
COOKBOOK
Lutefisk Surprise
1. take one lutefisk
2 get rid of it
ED FISCHER

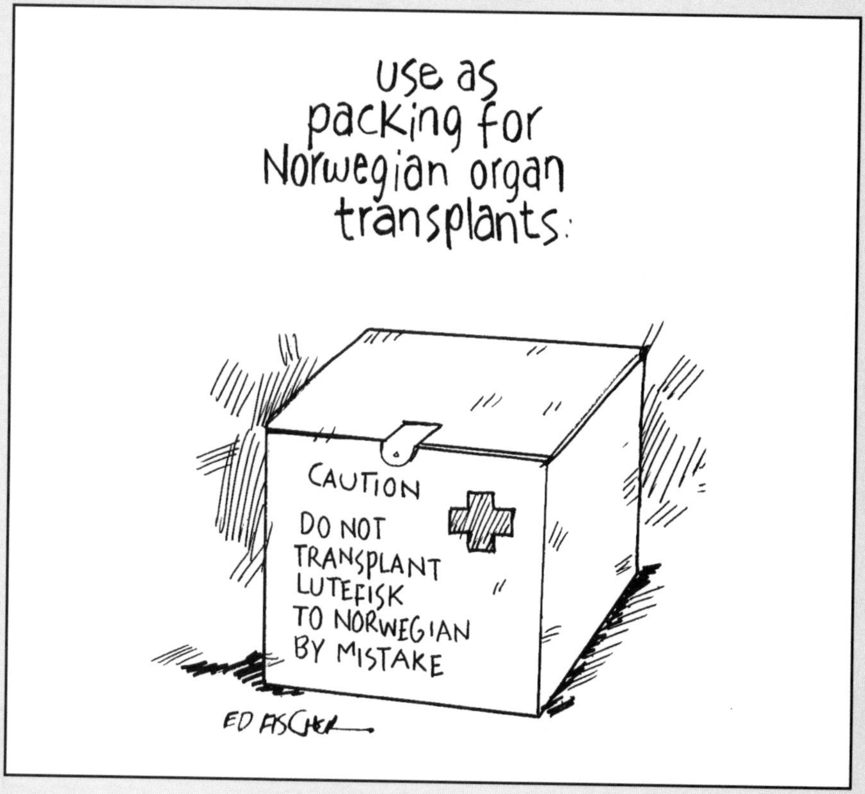
use as packing for Norwegian organ transplants:
CAUTION
DO NOT TRANSPLANT LUTEFISK TO NORWEGIAN BY MISTAKE
ED FISCHER

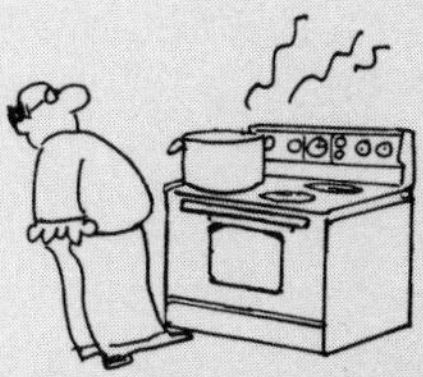

As a joke, James (Jammy) Johanson of New Oslo, Minnesota, gift-wrapped lutefisk to give his wife for their wedding anniversary. As a joke, his wife locked the bedroom door for two weeks.

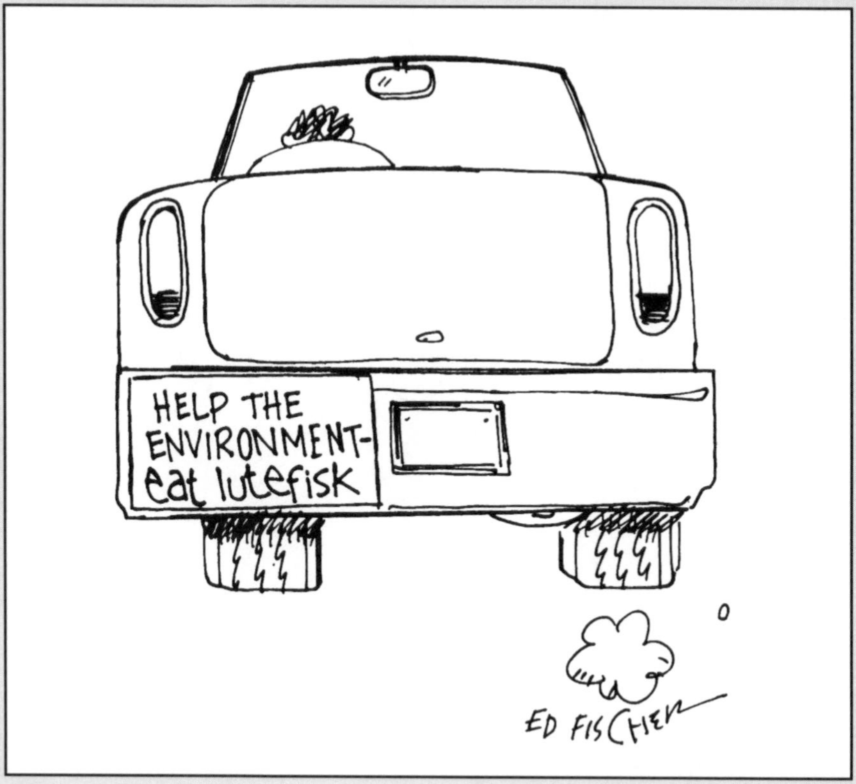
HELP THE
ENVIRONMENT-
eat lutefisk
ED FISCHER

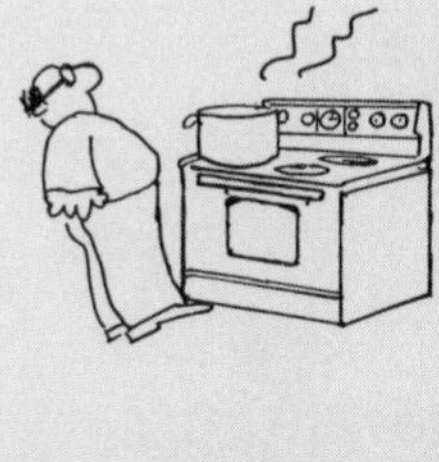

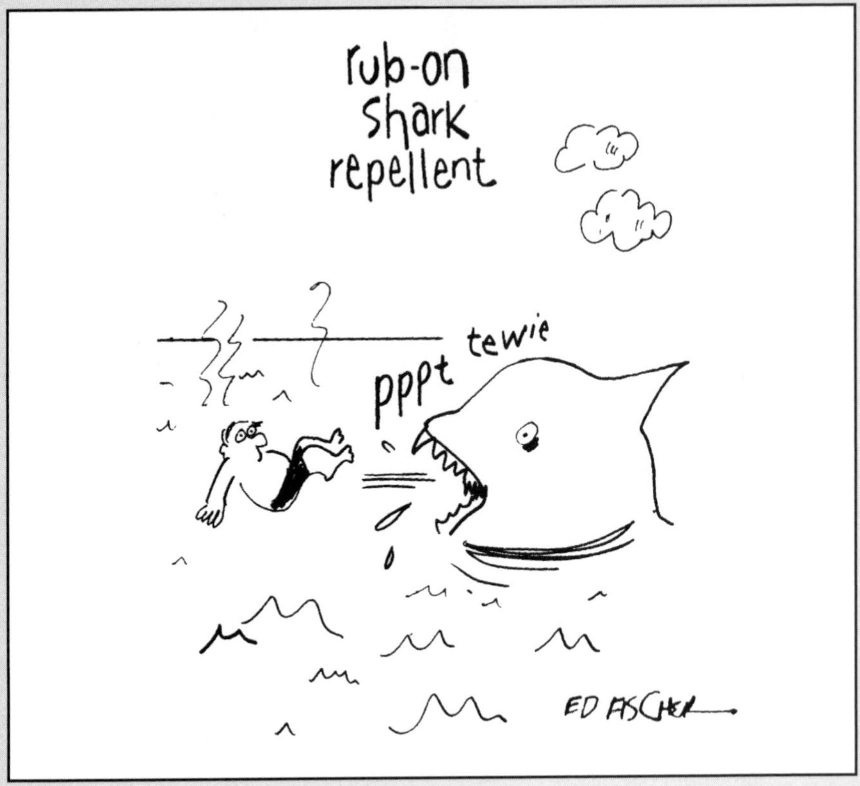
rub-on
shark
repellent
pppt
tewie
ED FISCHER

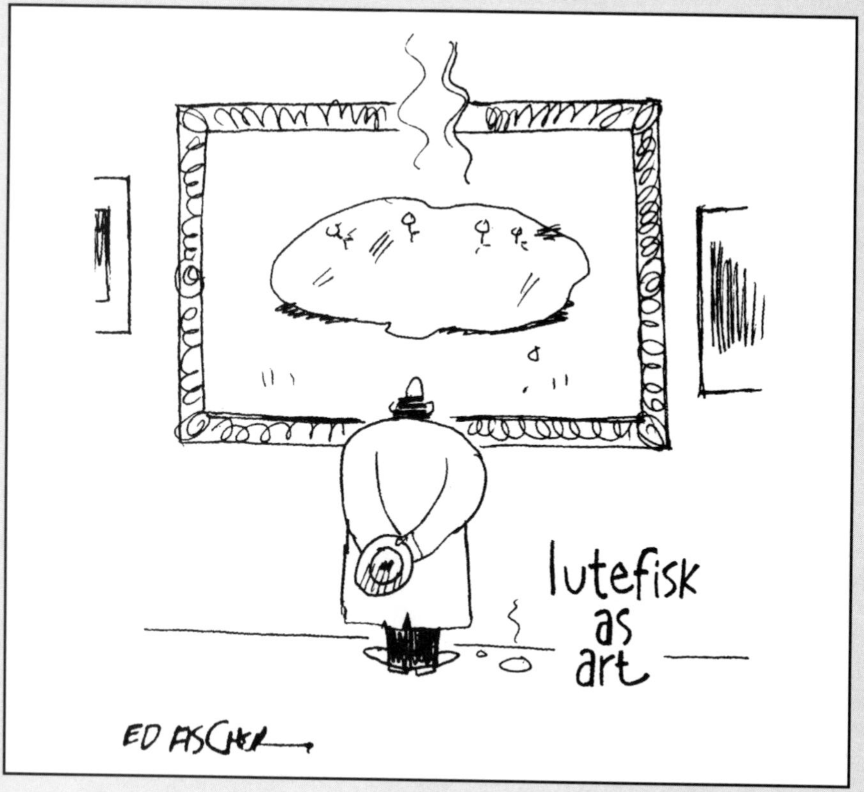
lutefisk
as
art
ED FISCHER

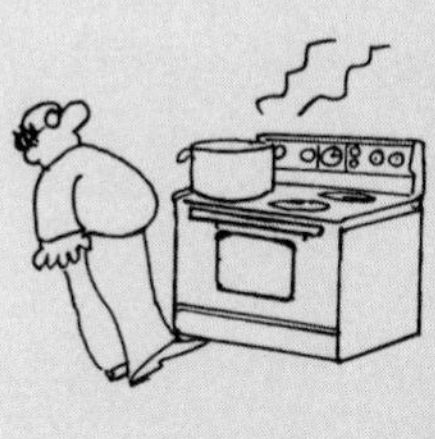

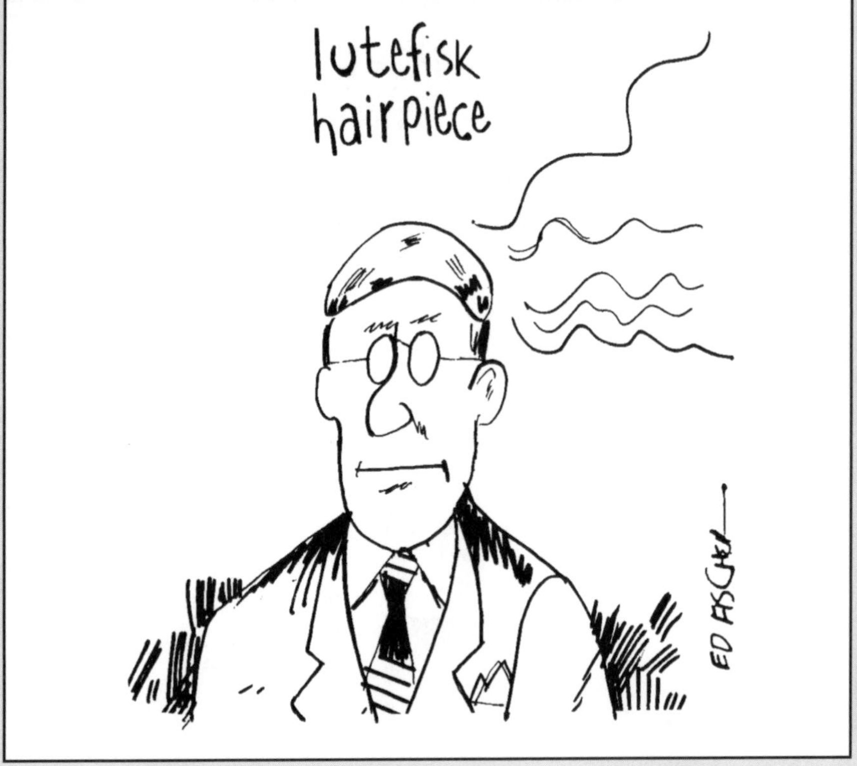
lutefisk
hairpiece
ED FISCHER

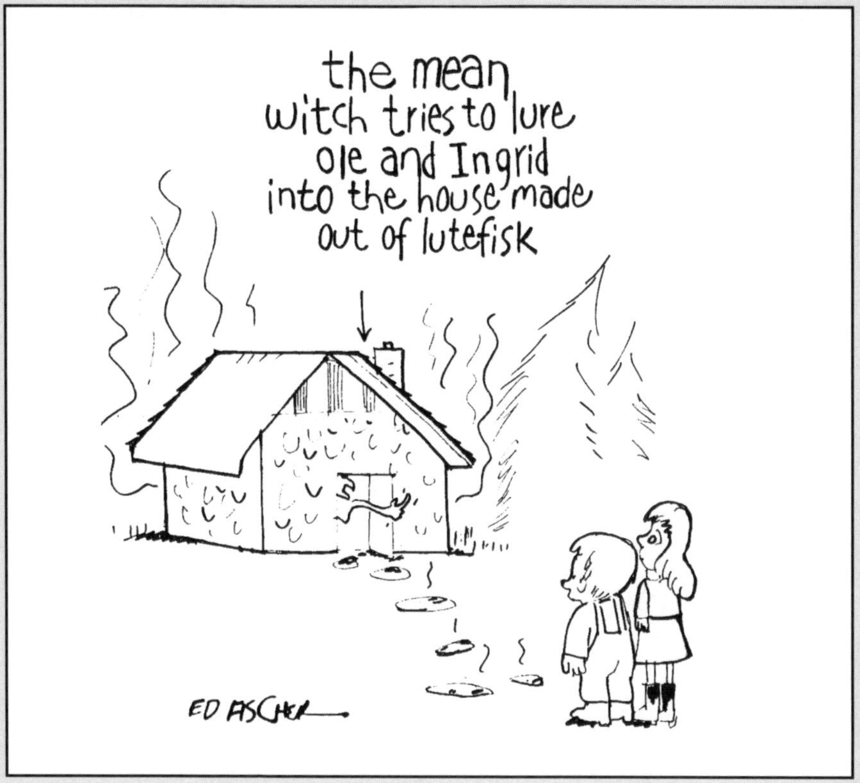
the mean
witch tries to lure
ole and Ingrid
into the house made
out of lutefisk
ED FISCHER

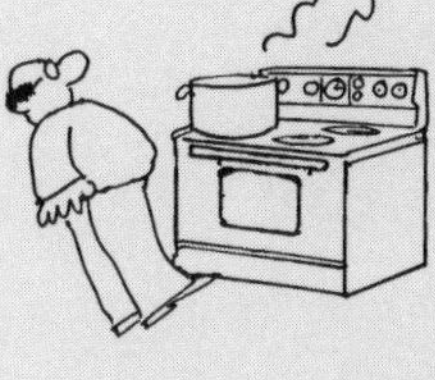

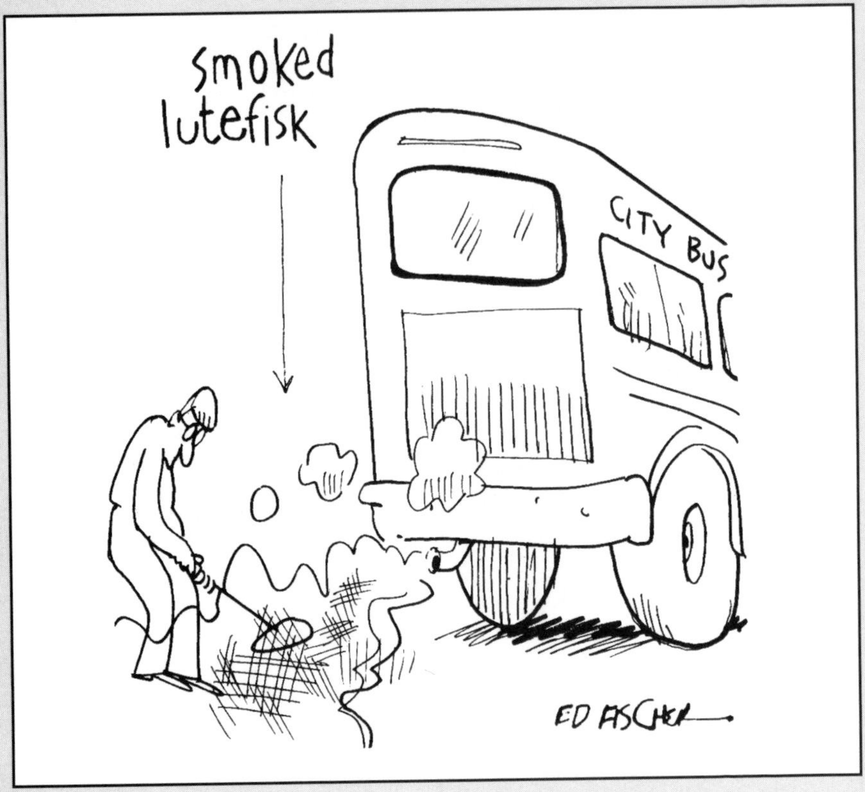
smoked
lutefisk
CITY BUS
ED FISCHER

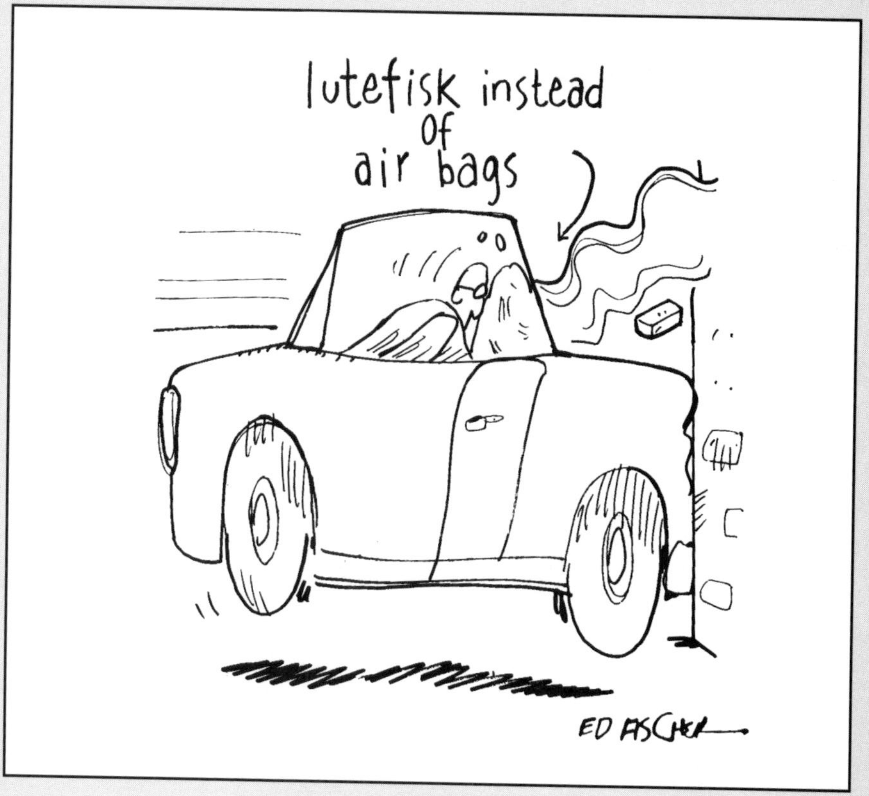
lutefisk instead of air bags
ED FISCHER

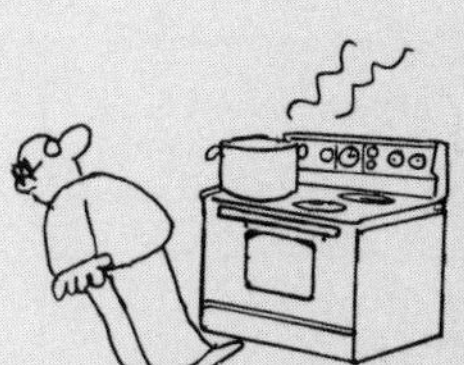

Astrid Olaffson of Pueck, Minnesota, says one of her most memorable vacations was the time she and some friends were stranded in a cabin during a blizzard with nothing to eat for two weeks but lutefisk. "It was great," she said. "Everyone lost over ten pounds"

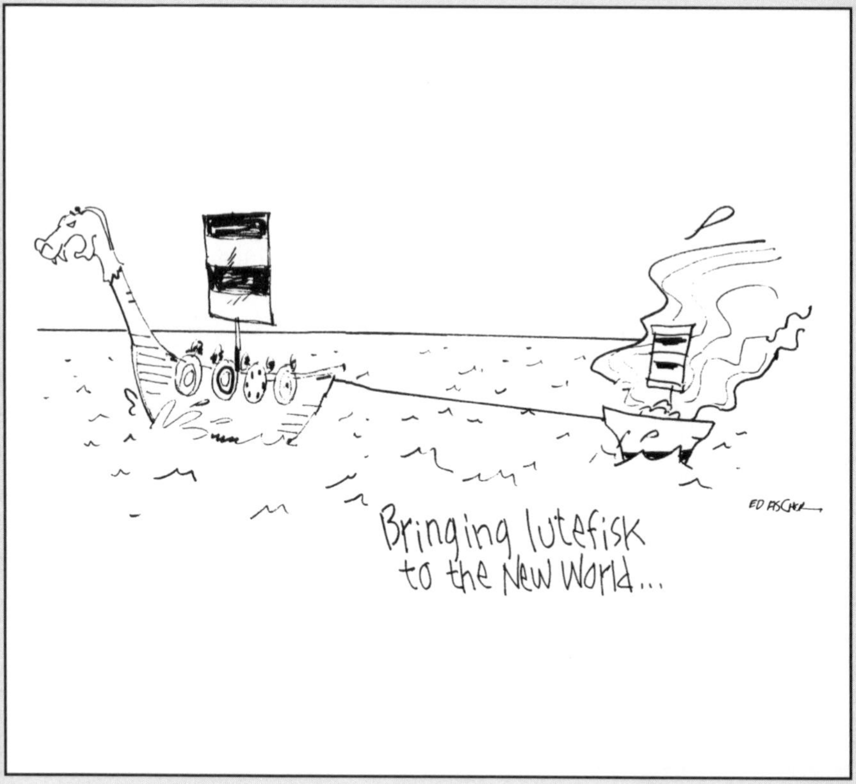
Bringing lutefisk
to the New World...
ED FISCHER

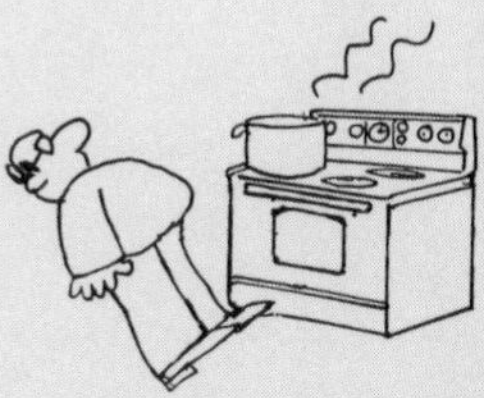

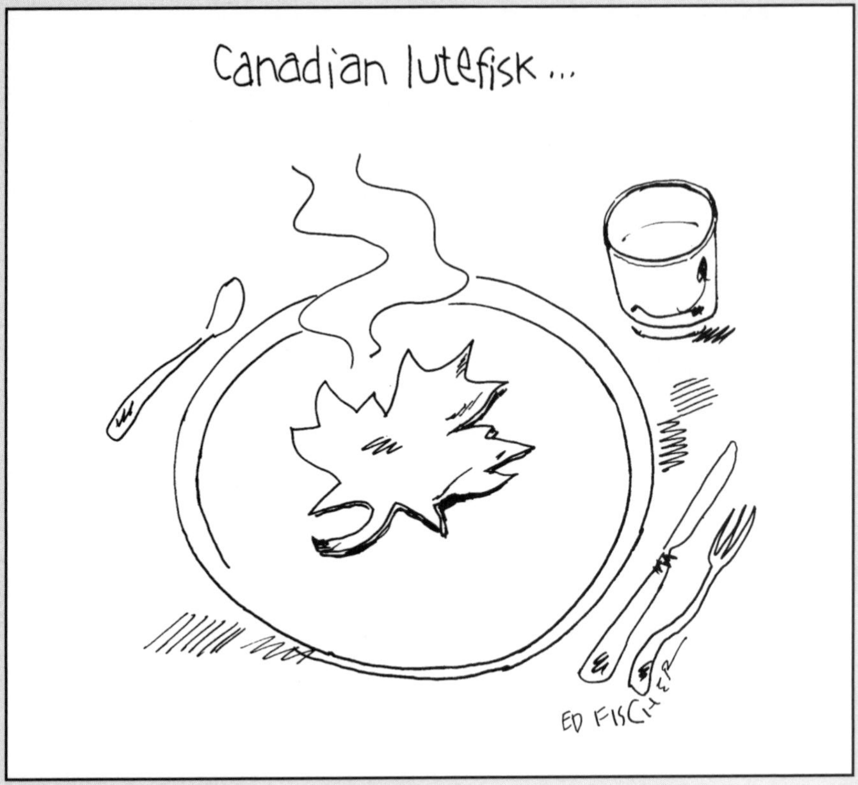
Canadian lutefisk...
ED FISCHER

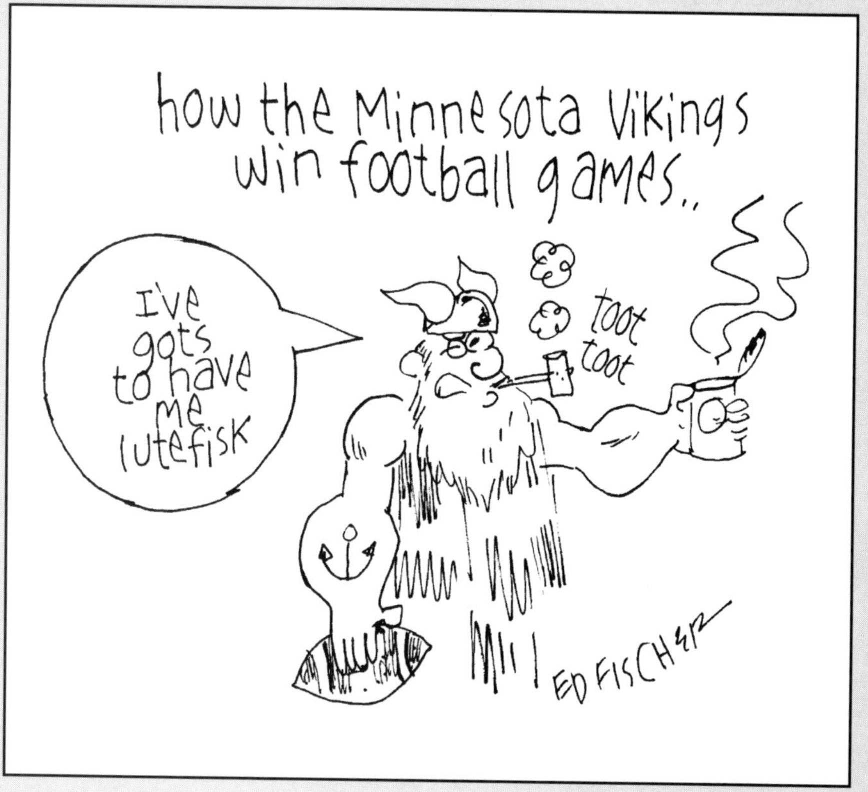
how the Minnesota Vikings win football games..
I've gots to have me lutefisk
toot toot
ED FISCHER

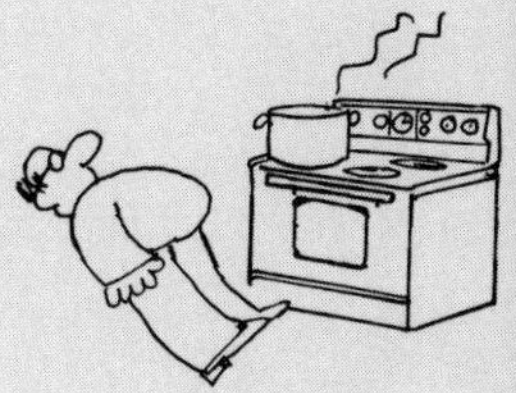

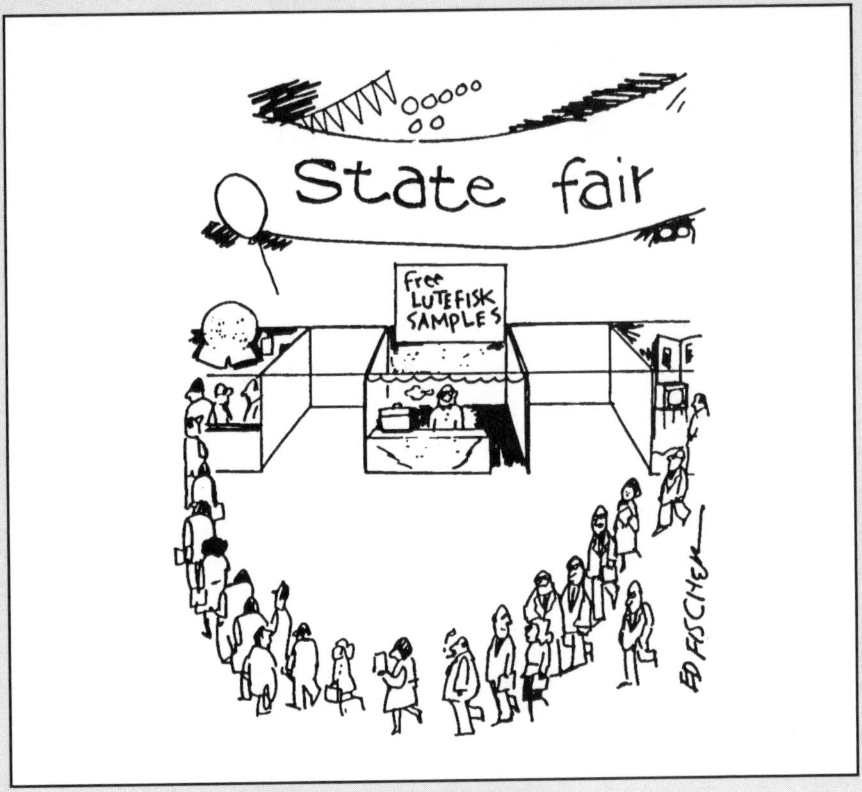
State fair
Free LUTEFISK SAMPLES
ED FISCHER

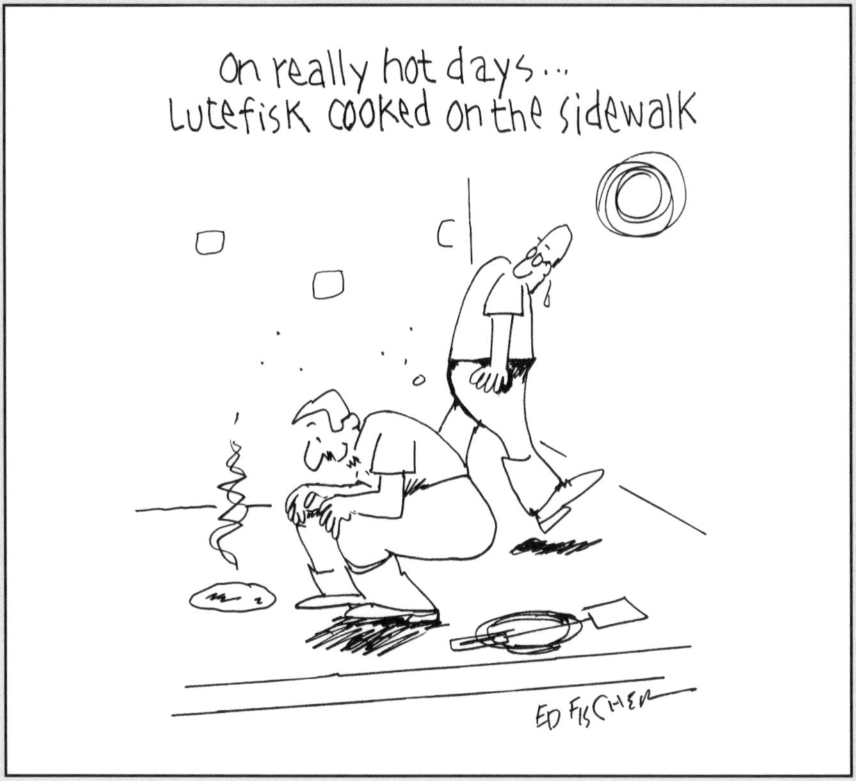
On really hot days...
Lutefisk cooked on the sidewalk
ED FISCHER

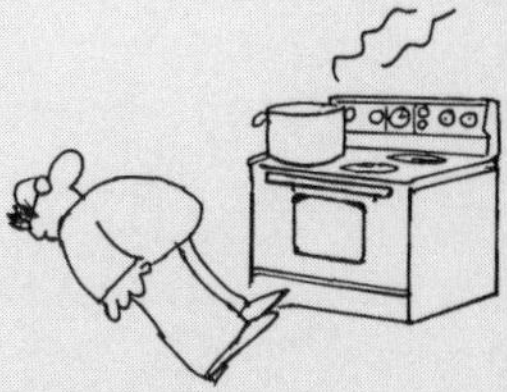

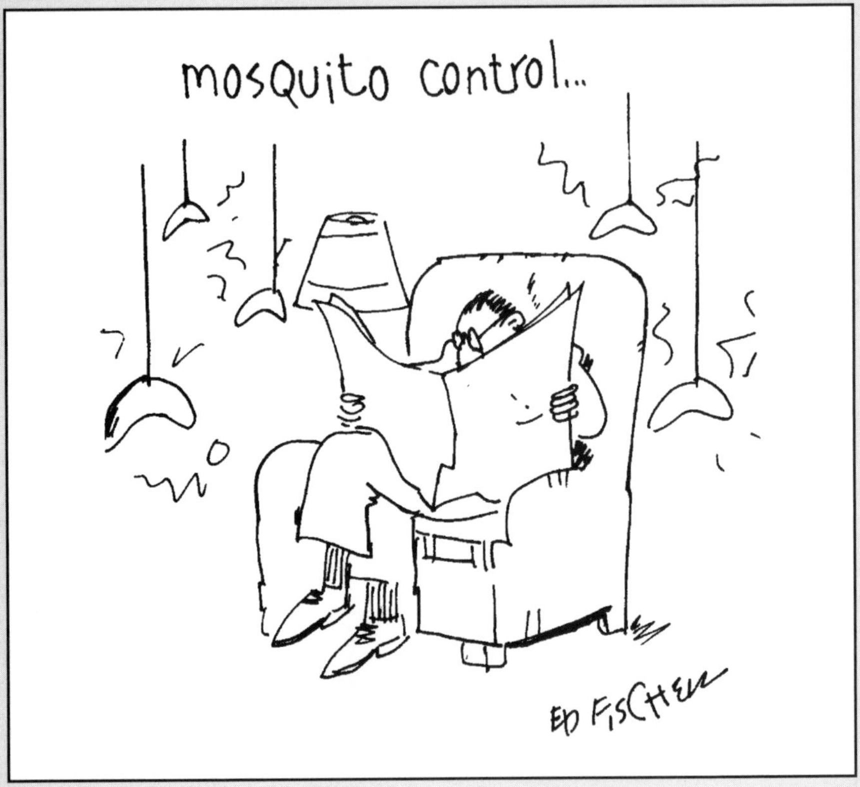
mosquito control...
ED FISCHER

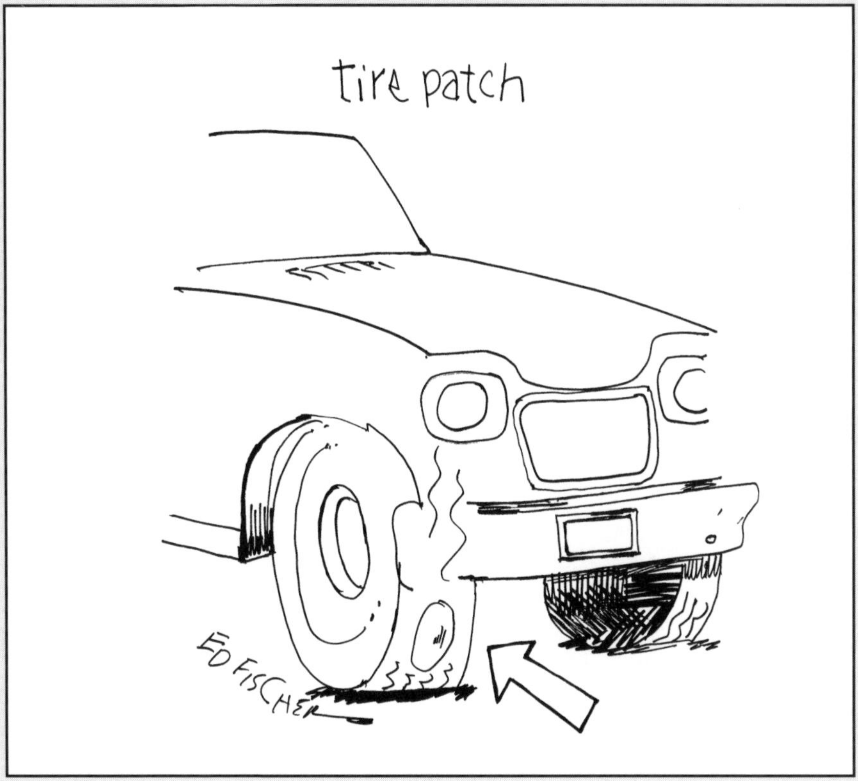
tire patch
ED FISCHER

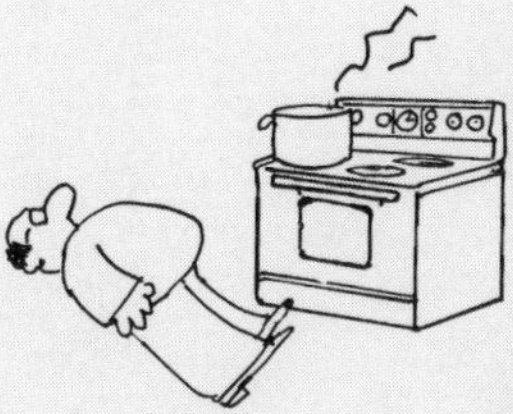

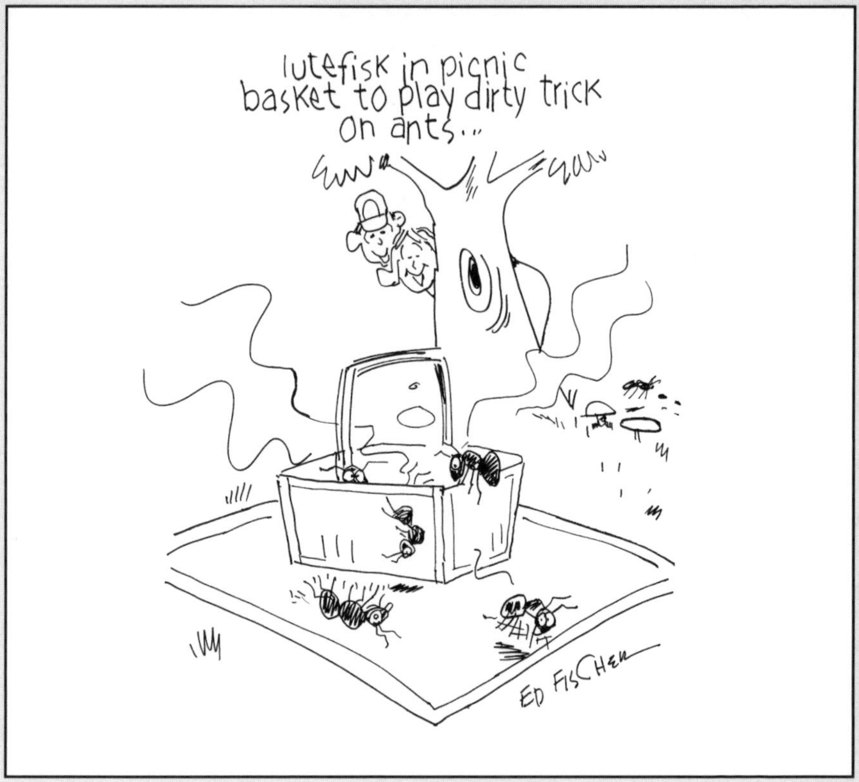
lutefisk in picnic
basket to play dirty trick
on ants...
ED FISCHER

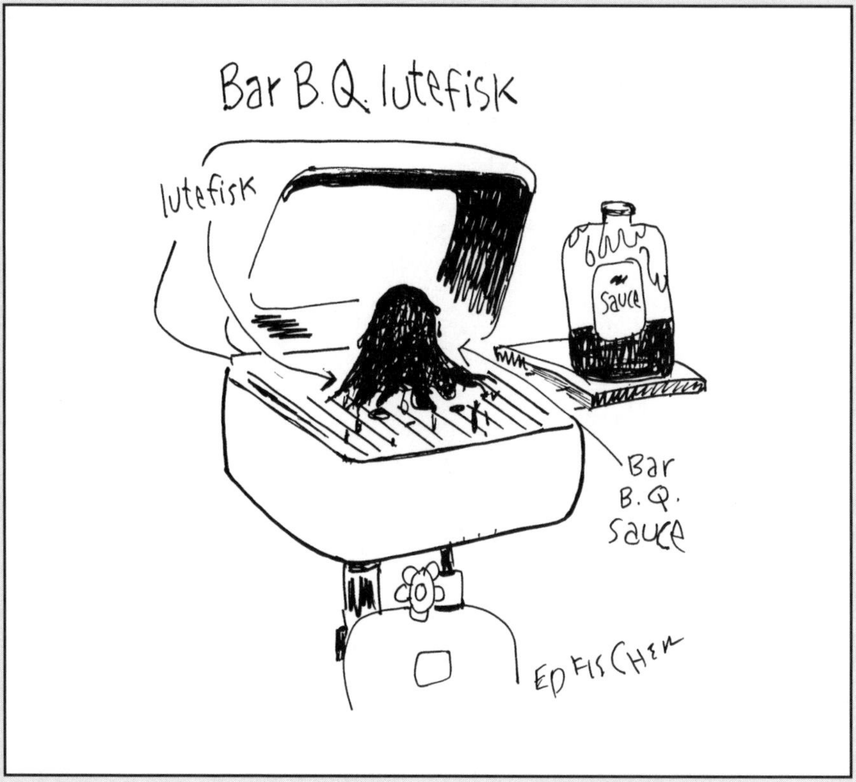
Bar B.Q. lutefisk
lutefisk
Sauce
Bar B.Q. sauce
ED FISCHER

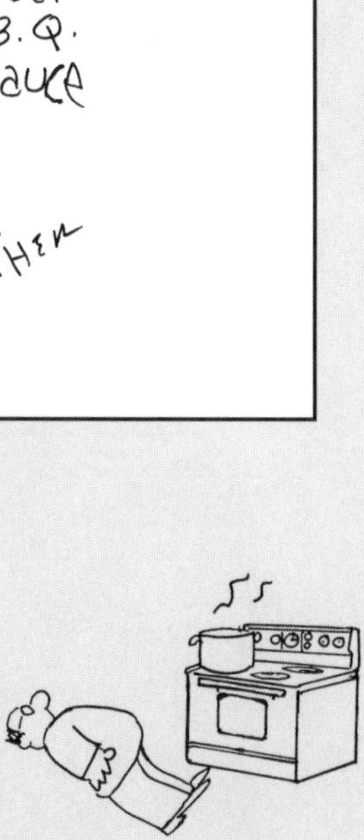

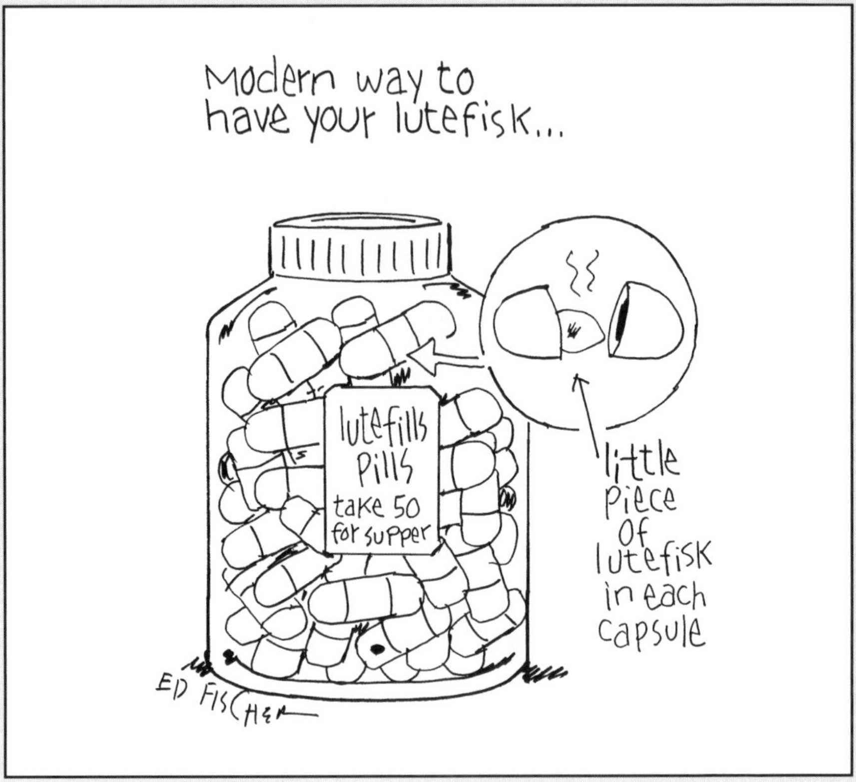
Modern way to have your lutefisk...
lutefills pills
take 50 for supper
little piece of lutefisk in each capsule
ED FISCHER

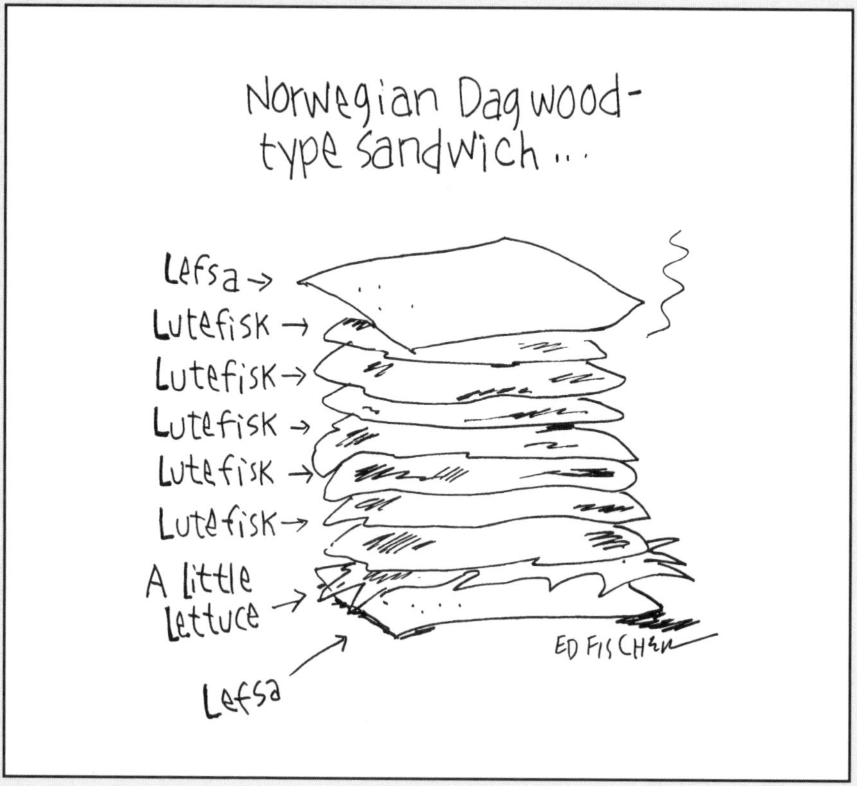
Norwegian Dagwood-
type Sandwich...
Lefsa →
Lutefisk →
Lutefisk →
Lutefisk →
Lutefisk →
Lutefisk →
A little lettuce →
Lefsa
ED FISCHER

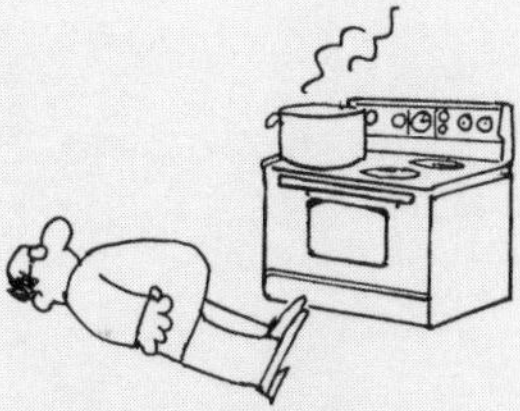

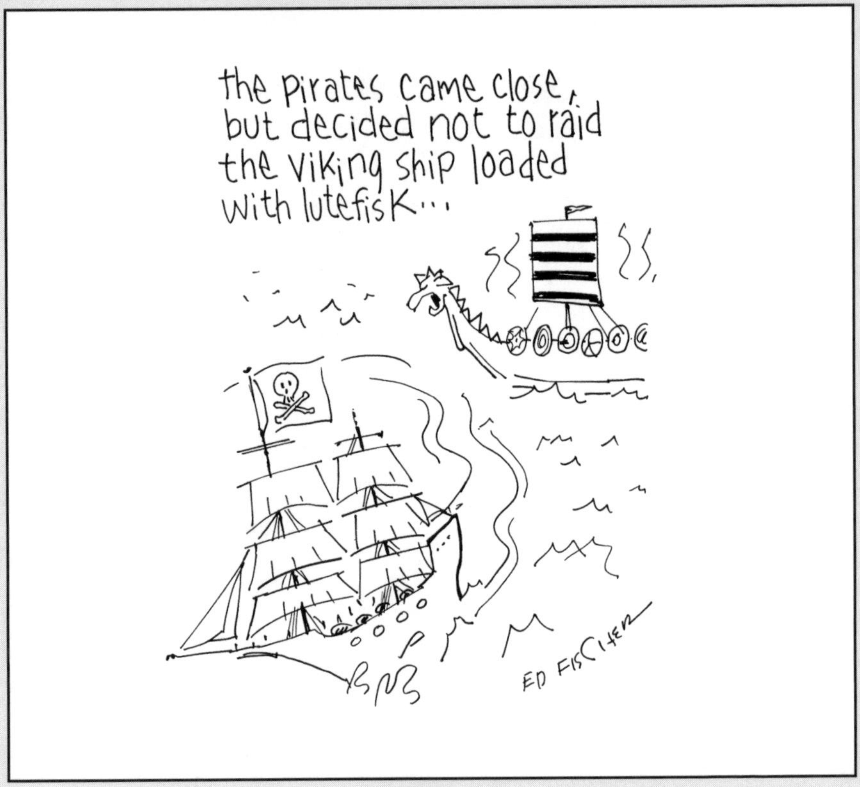
the pirates came close,
but decided not to raid
the viking ship loaded
with lutefisk...
ED FISCHER

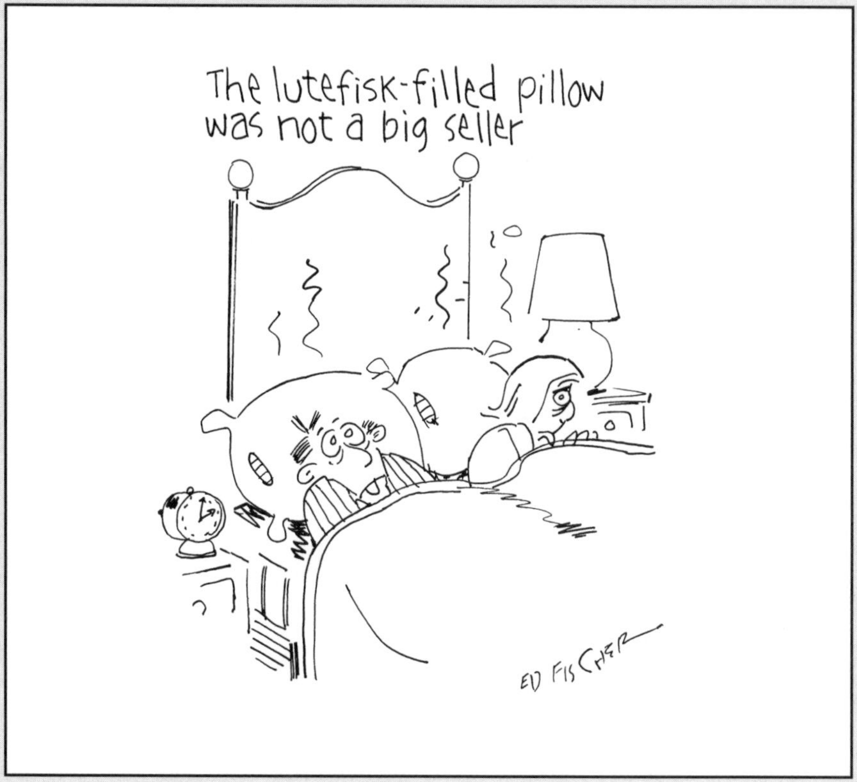
The lutefisk-filled pillow
was not a big seller
ED FISCHER

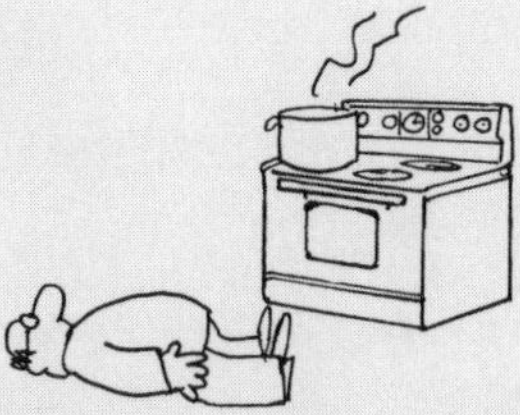

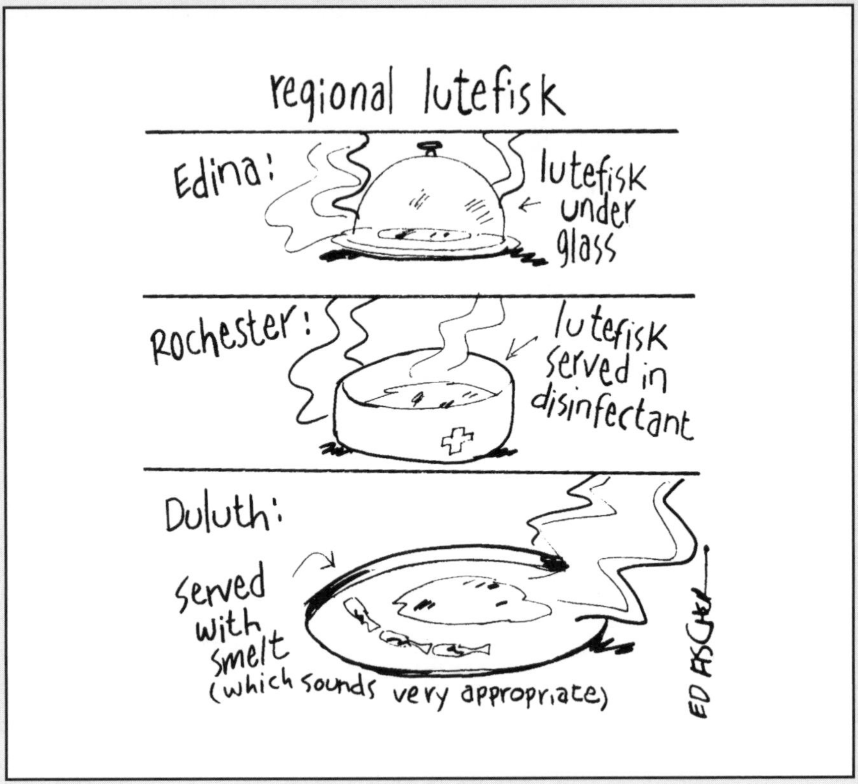
regional lutefisk
Edina:
lutefisk under glass
Rochester:
lutefisk served in disinfectant
Duluth:
served with smelt (which sounds very appropriate)
ED FISCHER

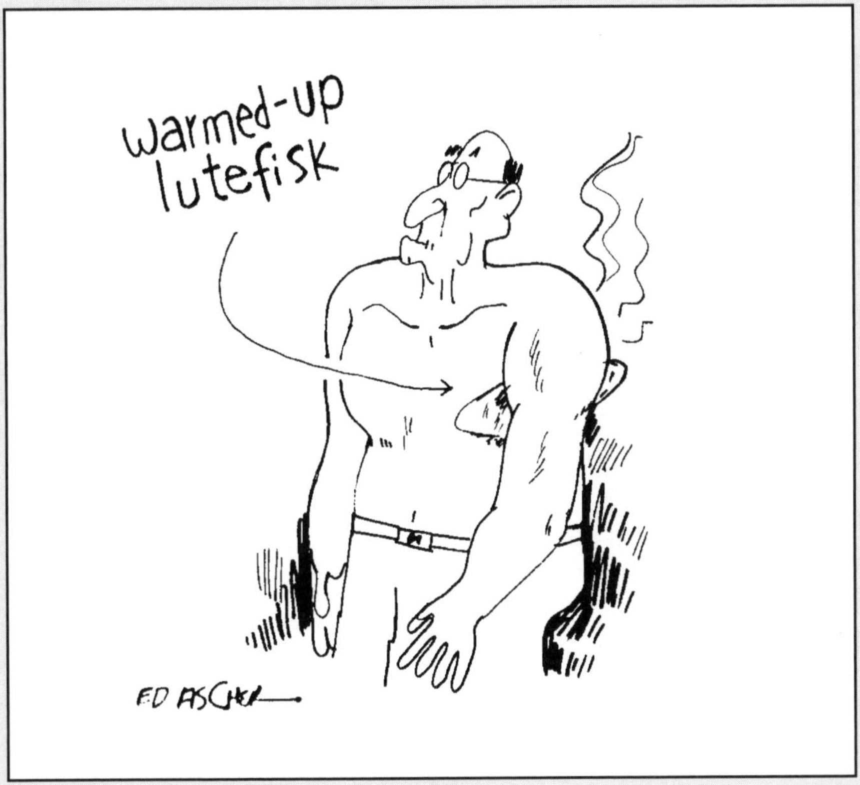
warmed-up lutefisk
ED FISCHER

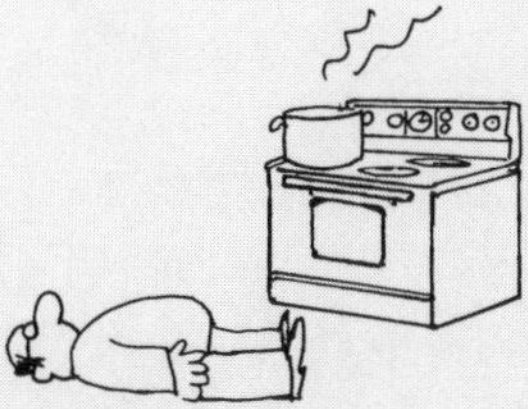

Several hundred Girl Scouts in south Minneapolis spent a month going door to door selling Girl Scout lutefisk instead of Girl Scout cookies. They feel they would have sold a lot of lutefisk, but nobody was home.

ED FISCHER

UFF DA UFF DA UFF DA

91

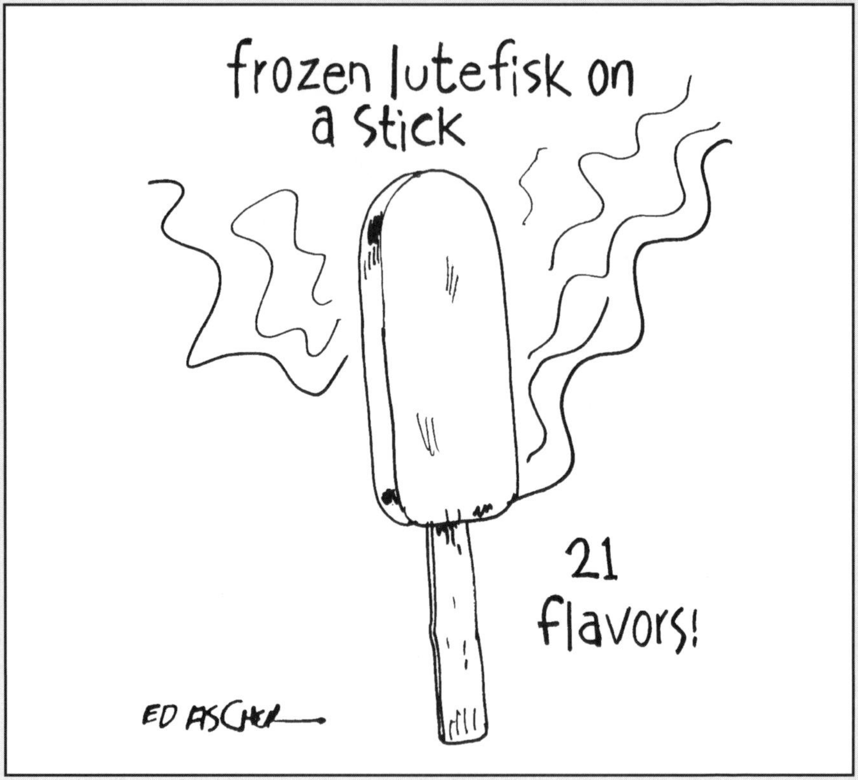
frozen lutefisk on
a Stick
21
flavors!
ED FISCHER

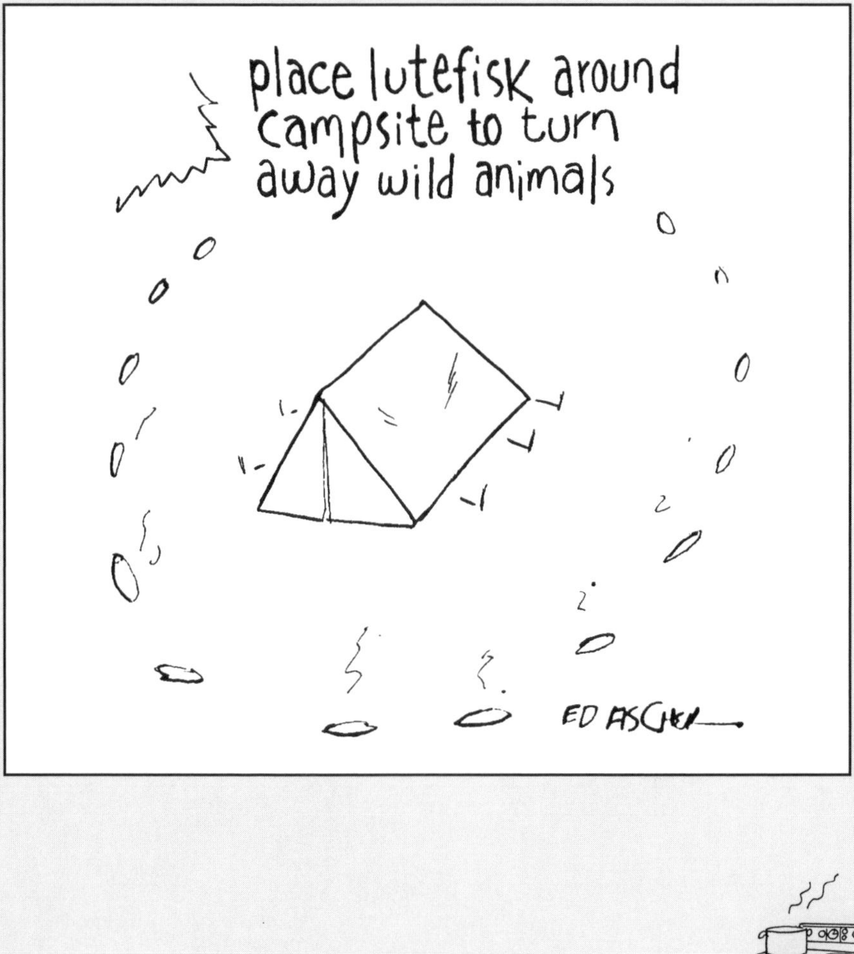
place lutefisk around campsite to turn away wild animals
ED FISCHER

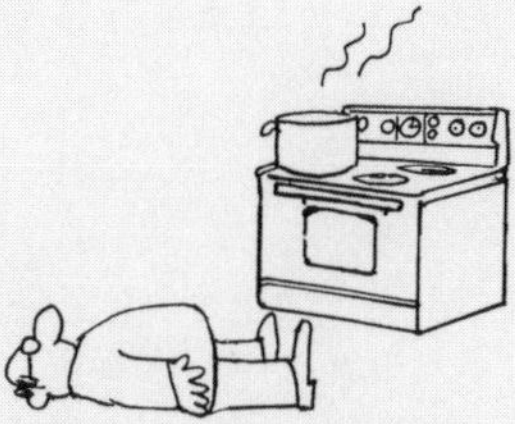

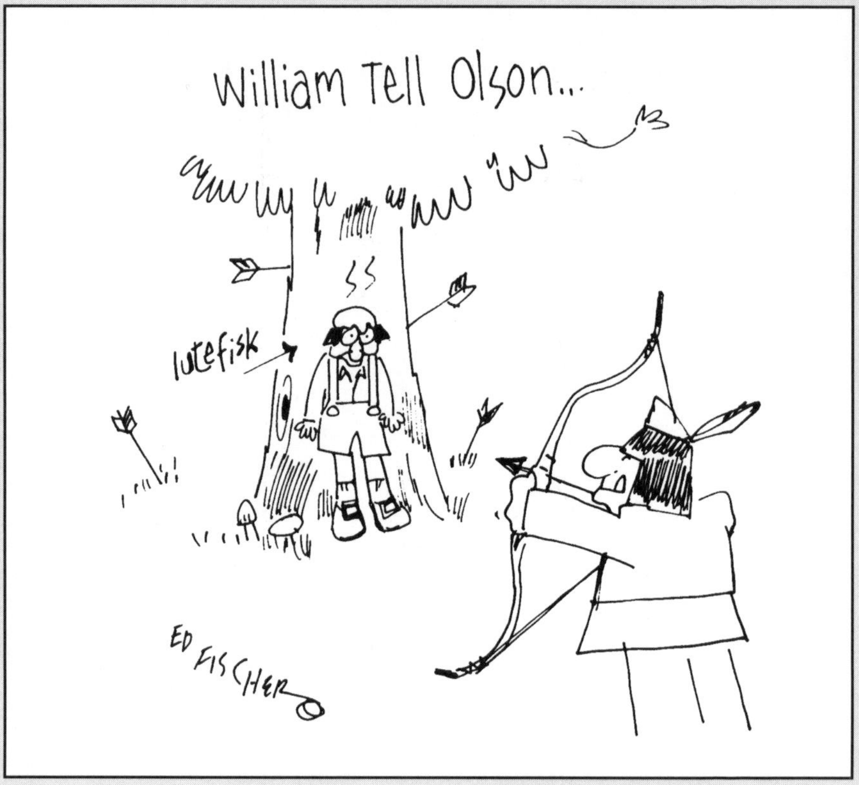
William Tell Olson...
lutefisk
ED FISCHER

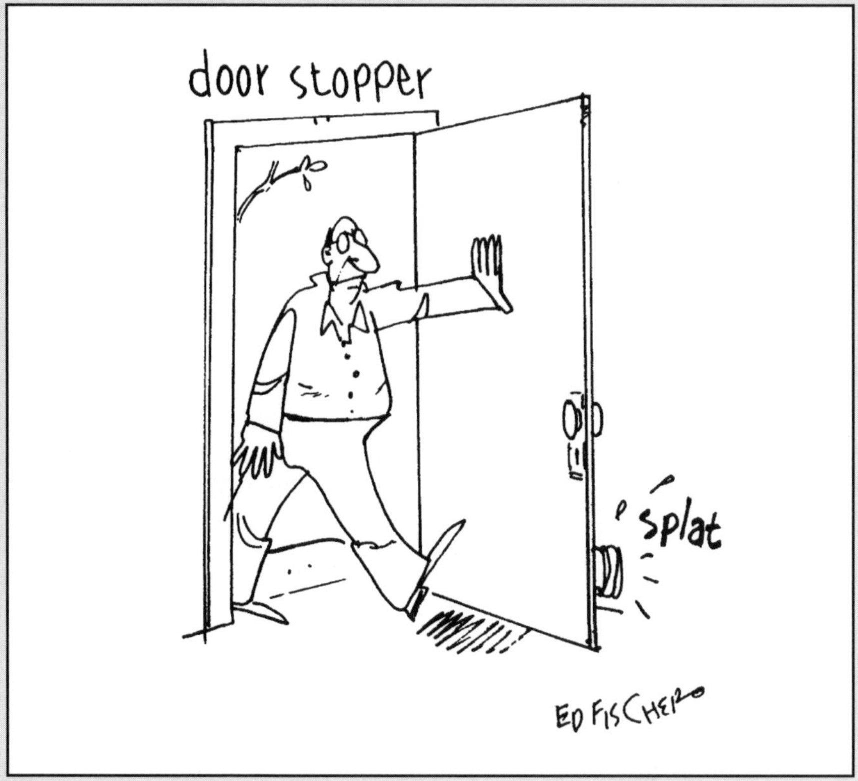
door stopper
splat
ED FISCHER

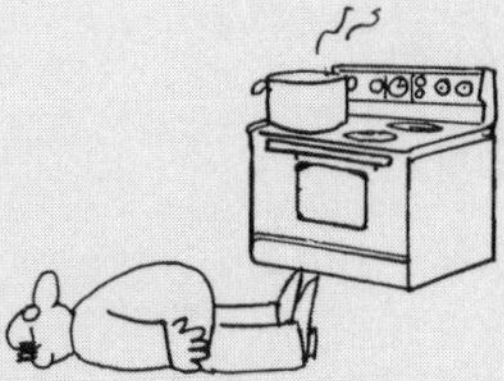

Lutefisk: Scandinavian dish made from cod soaked in lye for an extended period of time, or by some modern, scientific method, and usually prepared at holidays of on special occasions. Gets its unique aroma from being cooked. Sprinkle with warm memories and serve with love.